ERNIE PYLE'S SOUTHWEST

Illustrated by Bob Bales

Trail-Notes by Ed Ainsworth

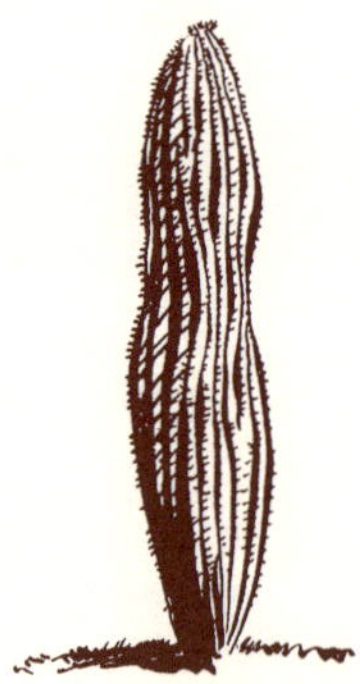

with special appreciation to
my friend, Ed Ainsworth
and the Desert-Southwest Publishers

The Southwest Desert

It was before WW II. Ernie pointed to the Western skyline saying, "Bob, that mountain ridge must be 50 miles from here, can you imagine that?" We are standing in his new front year that had no grass (yet) and at a new tract house out near the airport. "Uncle Shag" as he was known to me, was right proud of my being an artist, now enroute to the big war. During my two day visit, he asked me to paint a border around his one bathroom with some blue and black paint he had. He wanted nautical subjects, being a Navy reservist. That little house on Gerard Street is now a museum/monument to my mentor, Ernest Taylor Pyle. He treated me like I was really famous and laughed at my stories. He had a lot to do with my future since bringing me and my mother home from the hospital when I was born some years earlier. He's gone now, but his little desert house still stands proudly in the hot Albuquerque sun, which made Ernie feel good.

by Bob Bales

PART ONE

FAR PLACES

If you choose to wander off the beaten track, you're liable to find almost anything, from squashy sand to good old gumbo and, worst of all, worn-out gravel full of millions of holes.

. . . Ernie Pyle

Roads were bad or non-existent in many parts of the Southwest when Ernie Pyle made his expeditions into the realm of solitude. Depression was gripping the nation in 1935 and on through 1939, the period covered by these columns. He had been saddened by the sight of penniless Americans selling apples, desperately seeking work, drifting from one state to another, blinded by grit in the Dust Bowl, beset by cold and hunger in the big cities. Ernie Pyle was seeking solace, not alone for himself but for all Americans. He was a vicarious emissary of the destitute dreaming of a Valhalla in the Promised Land. He thought the Promised Land, as of old, might be in the Desert. That is where he searched for it.

Introduction to FAR PLACES by Ed Ainsworth

Sometimes a man's most enduring memorial is built in the heart of a child who hero-worships him. This is a monument of the mind, a cenotaph of the spirit, subject neither to erosion nor the destructive fury of the elements. It is timeless.

So when a boy on the banks of the Wabash idolized a man who was to become the most beloved columnist of his era there was created a memorial which would outlast Death itself.

This memorial is to Ernie Pyle, newspaperman supreme, whose mortal life was snuffed out by a Japanese bullet during World War II, but whose words live on, and now are reborn with pictorial adornment by the hand of that hero-worshiping boy of long ago, now a man himself.

Lt. Colonel George C. (Bob) Bales, once "the favorite nephew"—although never any blood kin—of Ernie Pyle in the Wabash River country of Western Indiana has drawn the illustrations for this volume dealing with an enduring facet of Ernie Pyle's life in his beloved Southwest.

This is the story of Ernie Pyle as he saw the land.

Many still think of Ernie almost entirely as the war correspondent who, through his courage and his understanding words, became the favorite not only of the public at home in the United States but also of the fighting men everywhere on far-flung battlefronts. Yet Ernie was world-famous for human, down-to-earth, sensitive columns about men, women, children and places long before World War II. And his love for the solitary places of the Southwest was part of his nature.

For years, in his descriptions of the people he knew, Ernie Pyle wrote about his "Aunt Mary" in Indiana, who had helped rear him. "Aunt Mary" became known to millions of Ernie's readers; his affection illuminated every word he wrote about her.

"Aunt Mary" was Mrs. Mary Bales, grandmother of Bob Bales.

The Pyle family and the Bales family lived close to each other south of the town of Dana, near Webster's Creek and about seven miles from the Wabash River.

To Bob Bales it was a source of never-ending fascination that the Pyle home was built atop a T-shaped Indian Mound. Every once in a while arrowheads and pieces of pottery would turn up, to the delight of Bob and his older brother Jack.

Equally fascinating to the boys was the glamorous Ernie Pyle who, when Bob was 12 or 13, already was beginning to achieve fame as a newspaperman. Ernie himself, as a boy, had been almost constantly at Aunt Mary's house, and he was known to Bob Bales from infancy. Ernie always said that Bob was his favorite "nephew" and that he would grow up to be a famous artist. To help this goal along, Ernie gave Bob his first set of paints.

Ernie watched with pride the increasing facility of Bob Bales as an artist, although he did not live to see him become Lt. Colonel George C. Bales, pilot, navigator, painter, and official head of the U. S. Air Force's Art program throughout the world. Yet this was to be one of the climaxing achievements of Colonel Bales, who gathered a pictorial history of the Air Force in more than 2000 paintings by the finest painters on earth for public display and for the Air Force Academy at Colorado Springs.

Ernie Pyle's little box of paints was prophetic.

That was the kind of discernment Ernie possessed.

It is no wonder, in turn, that out of boyhood hero-worship and later enduring friendship with Ernie as a man that Bob Bales has felt impelled to give supplemental expression in pictorial form to that sometimes-neglected phase of Ernie Pyle's life in the Southwest.

Ernie sought sanctuary in the wilds.

He found balm in solitude.

Bob Bales has caught this spirit. Ernie and he offer it, as a distillation and gift of the years, to you.

Footsteps sounded a little while ago on the Imperishable Trail.

They were not very loud. He who made them was a slight man and he walked gently on the earth.

Yet the sound of these footsteps has swelled with the years in the Land of the Imperishable. They have become imperishable themselves. At first they were like the little sound of an Indian drum in the night, the throb of a heartbeat against the sky. Then they grow to the thunder of a big drum, echoing to the distant white moon across the canyon of time.

Ernie Pyle was the man who walked here.

It was in the Imperishable Land that Ernie Pyle felt a kinship, felt at home. He built himself a house and he wrote imperishably of the people and their dreams in the lonely vastness.

This was in the place they call the Southwest. At the heart of it is the spot named Albuquerque.

It is the Land of the Imperishable because it is compounded of the things that endure.

Zuni silver shines bright under the sun. The turquoise from the veins of the earth is like the sky at noon. The schist and the granite are piled up high and they defy the ravages of lightning and the black storms. In the thin air the smell of woodsmoke is forever present as if persisting from the days when men lived in caves and marveled at the discovery of fire.

Upreared in lonely and massive dignity are the ancient mesas. In isolation on the tops of some of them live the Hopis, dwelling with their immemorial fetishes as if rooted in eternity. From their eyries they gaze with the eyes of eagles across a jagged and never-changing world to the edge of vision.

Yonder, too, are the Navajos, the allies of silence. Their hogans cling stubbornly to the buffeted land, unmindful of change and dedicated to loneliness.

The earth and the heavens complement each other. Men here get a closer view of infinity. The human soul is dwarfed by the contemplation of the distant unknown, abashed by the mighty avenues of the stars.

In this Land of the Imperishable, of all places on earth, Ernie Pyle felt most in tune with the Almighty.

To his receptive soul came the disclosure of the simple yet terrifying complex workings of Nature.

Here the waters are separated by the Continental Divide for their wanderings to the sea.

Snow and rain beget tiny tributaries of the Colorado to launch their Westward journey through the awesome depths of the Grand Canyon to the Sea of Cortez.

This is where the Rio Grande begins.

Its little drops of water start bravely in this sometimes cold upland. They grow in volume, like Ernie Pyle's words, and set their course for the south and for the liquid syllables of distant Mexican villages and at last the caressing warmth of the distant Gulf.

These phenomena, these mysteries, these workings of the infinite terrify some men.

They never terrified Ernie Pyle.

He was in tune with rain and wind and sun and heat and cold and mirages and the songs of the treetops.

Somehow, too, amid the great peaks and the mighty Saguaro cactus reaching their tortured arms to the sky, he sensed truly that the emotions of men are magnified just as the clear air of the Southwest magnifies distant objects.

Love is stronger. Hate is deeper. A common humanity, when it is evoked, is intensified.

So Ernie Pyle found it to be in the far places.

He wandered without any definite purpose, seemingly, traveling over dim, rutted sand tracks; restlessly yearning for "the farthest place from nowhere." He never found it, of course; nobody does; but perhaps the yearning for it is the important thing. It gives a man depth to reach out his arms for the unattainable.

Along the Imperishable Trail, all things seemed to Ernie Pyle to bear the stamp of immortality. The eagles in the heavens appeared to have been there forever. The gale-lashed trees at timberline, ragged and gnarled, bore the mark of eternity. Even the deer and coyotes, transient as they seem in habitats closer to man, walked in the highlands of the Southwest as if they were endowed with everlasting qualities.

These things caused Ernie Pyle to ponder.

He weighed the secrets of life in the far places in the balances of his mind. He sought answers to riddles of Nature. He basked in the sunlight of a widening mental horizon; he found, even when there was no articulate answer from the wilderness, some balm in the silences which surrounded him.

In his writings, then, Ernie Pyle captured the Imperishables. The words live beyond him. They bespeak his spirit. And his spirit itself is Imperishable.

—Ed Ainsworth

ERNIE VISITS THE OLD MAN OF THE MOUNTAIN

*PHOENIX, Ariz.–

There are many little incidents on an 8000-mile drive in a strange country. Incidents that, thought back upon, give you a chuckle, or send a warm feeling thru your heart, or make you mad.

Such incidents, for example, as that of the old man on the mountain. It was in northwestern Arizona, when we left the dirt road and struck out thru the cactus toward a gold mine up on the mountain side.

When we got there, after much bumping and twisting, we found the mine was not working. But we found an old man living there, in a one-room shack, all alone except for his dog. The dog, a friendly little collie, was called, of all things for the desert, "Toodles."

The man was 72, bareheaded, his whiskers were white, he wore a plaid flannel shirt and clean overalls. We thought he looked fine, but he apologized all over the place for his appearance. He got out his keys and took us thru the idle ore mill, explained the dust-covered machinery.

He had been right there on that very spot for 22 years. When the mine was running he worked there. When it closed, he stayed on as watchman. He just gathers wood and cooks his meals, and watches. He doesn't see very many people. I don't know what he will do when his little dog dies. She has saved his life twice, by warning him of rattlesnakes in the cabin. She barks differently when she sees a snake.

One of the first things he asked was what day it was. We told him Thursday. "That's what I thought," he said. "This is the day for the stage." Twice a week, he said, he walks down the road (four miles each way) to meet the stage. It brings him groceries and mail, so he said. We watched it go by while we were there, a white truck far down the mountainside. We were going to take him down if it stopped. We three stood there with our eyes shaded, watching the truck for 10 minutes. But it didn't stop. "Nothing for me today, I guess," he said. Some day I'm going to send him a post card, so the stage driver will have something to stop for.

He was so glad we came. He stood and waved to us till we were far away.

*Ernie Pyle's columns in this book first appeared in the Washington News and Scripps-Howard newpapers and some of them later were included in the book "Home Country" (William Sloane Associates). They were copyrighted 1935, 1936, 1937, 1938, 1939, 1940, 1942 and 1947 by Scripps-Howard Newspaper Alliance and by William Sloane Associates, Inc., and are used through their courtesy and permission.

Then there was the night when, after miles of driving over dirt roads thru swirling snow, we came to a little town.

The hotel was a Fred Harvey hotel, right in the railroad station. But, as cold and miserable as we were, the price for a room was too high, and I asked the clerk if he had nothing cheaper.

"Yes," he said "There IS a room in the back of the hotel, but (and here I could imagine he drew himself up a little) it isn't a Harvey room."

Harvey room or no Harvey room we took it. It turned out to be a room for engineers on the Santa Fe, a very warm and very clean room. We liked the room very much, but I could never have told the clerk so. For he was a Harvey man.

The little town of Wickenburg, Ariz., advertises itself as the "dude ranch capital of the world."

At noon time in a greasy-spoon restaurant there, we saw three dude ranch guests and one "cowboy," their escort, having lunch.

The "cowboy" was dressed in a green gabardine uniform, in cut sort of a cross between cowboy's clothes and Mexican balcony-singer's. He was obviously synthetic.

One of the lady guests was full of whiskey and imagined her cowboy as a great big he-man. She was cooing and laying her head upon his great Hollywood breast. He seemed to enjoy it.

Phoenix and Tucson do not seem to me a part of the Southwest. They are too Chamber-of-Commerce, too resort. You might as well go to Miami Beach as to Tucson.

But the rest of the Southwest, from the Pecos to the Colorado, oh, what a country! It's ancient history—Santa Fe was a thriving village long before the Pilgrims ever heard of Plymouth Rock; its modern history—the wild days of mining and cattle raising are an epic probably not duplicated anywhere in the world; its surface—the diverse and luxurious desert plants, beautiful in bloom, solemn and mysterious when bare; the land itself—spaceless, free, a land of humility and good taste. I love the Southwest.

– April 5, 1935

ERNIE IMPRESSED BY DAM

LAS VEGAS, Nev.—My interest in Boulder Dam has always been about on a level with my interest in, for example, prunes. It could take it or leave it. I had seen Boulder Dam in headlines. I knew it was somewhere in the West, I knew it was a lot of cement across a river . . . but beyond that I knew nothing and cared nothing .

But all this is changed now. I am a Boulder Dam fan. Information about Boulder Dam oozes out of me, as Mark Twain said, like otter-of-roses out of the otter. For I have seen it. It just happened to be in my way, so I took a look. And it turned out to the 12th or 13th wonder of the world.

Boulder Dam was started in 1931. They have had amazingly good luck with it. They say they are nearly three years ahead of schedule. The last of the cement in the dam proper was poured last month. It will take another year and a half to clear off all the temporary construction around it, and to build the power houses in the canyon at its base.

It will be the mightiest power project in the world. Behind the dam will form a lake 135 miles long. With average rainfall, it will take seven years for this lake to fill up.

Boulder Dam is across the Colorado River, which at that point divides Arizona and Nevada. The Colorado runs thru a bitter land. It is mountainous, dark brown, barren. You can see for scores of miles, and you see not a thing but a great savage loneliness all splattered with deep gulleys and rocks and twisted bare mountains.

At Boulder City, eight miles from the dam you start going down hill. You wind around and around, and keep getting lower and lower, all the time looking for some sign of the dam. Then suddenly you come around a corner and there it is, and it almost knocks your hat off.

Let me try to picture it for you. You've parked your car on a ledge, about 100 feet wide, with a wall along the edge. You're standing at the wall. From where you are to the floor of the canyon, almost straight down, is the distance from the top of the Washington Monument to the ground, and half as far again. Behind you to the west the mountain rises on up above you. You're looking east, right across the canyon. Over there, the canyon wall comes straight up even higher than your level, and then slants off back like a mountainside.

To your left, looking up the canyon, is the dam. You are just about on a level with the top of it. It is 727 feet high, and the biggest hunk of cement you or anybody else ever saw. On each side, where it is built right into the canyon wall for anchorage, you can hardly tell where cement ends and nature's rock begins.

The great dam is littered with scaffolding and machinery; men are swarming over it like flies; you look thru your glasses and see men walking along the almost perpendicular face of the dam, held only by ropes around their waists.

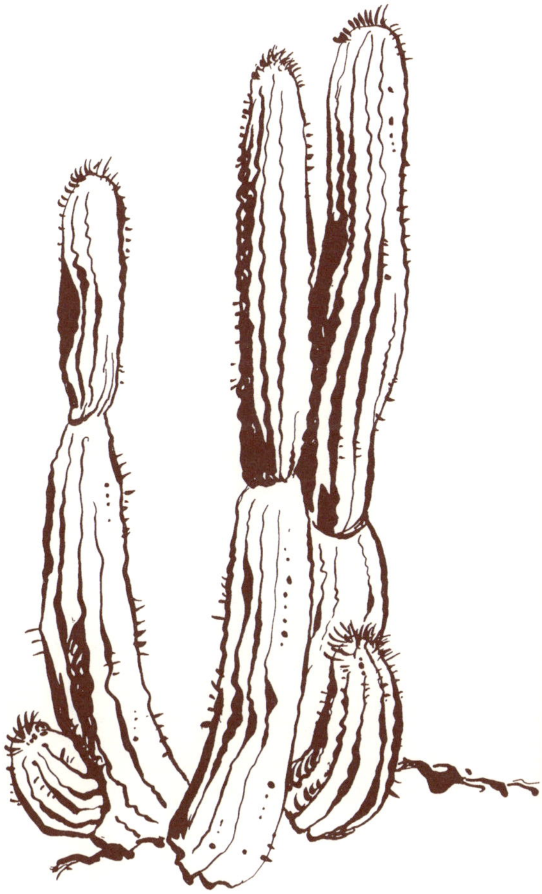

At the foot of the dam, and extending downstream toward you, are long cement buildings. By counting up, I figured they were about 14 stories high, yet from our perch on the ledge they seemed mere tool sheds. These are the power houses.

The entire floor of the canyon is a jumble of construction. Scores of men are working down there. You can see them move, but that is all. You have to use field glasses even to make sure they're men.

Across the canyon, from rim to rim, are stretched about a half dozen sets of cableways. One set is upstream from the dam. One is over it. Several are downstram. From these cables has descended all of Boulder Dam—the men, the machinery, the cement.

These cableways are the heart and soul of Boulder Dam. To me they were the most interesting thing there, and they seemed to typify the immensity of the whole unbelievable business.

The biggest cable will carry a 200-ton load. Here's an example of how it works. A truck, bearing a great hopper of cement, drives up on the ledge

where we stand, directly under the cable. A hook on the end of a steel line is let down from the carriage which runs back and forth across the great cable.

The hook is hooked onto the hopper of cement. High up on the hill, a man at the windlass pulls his lever, and the cement is drawn up to the carriage on the main cable. The man pulls another lever, and the carriage starts out across the canyon. Half way across it stops. Another lever. The 16-ton bucket of cement slowly descends into the depths of the canyon. You follow it with your glasses. You see where it's going. A large wooden framework, with a chute in the middle, sits on top of the powerhouses. Half a dozen men are there to receive the hopper and dump it. You see a man sitting down in one corner of the wooden framework. He has a telephone in his hand. He is telling the man at the windlass just how to swing the big bucket. The man at the windlass can no longer see it. Finally it arrives, and is dumped.

You look away for a moment. When you look back, you nearly fall over the cliff in astonishment. For the cable is coming back up, but it doesn't have the cement bucket on the the end. No, a man is there! He stands with one foot on the hook, the other hanging in the air, one arm around the cable. You sand rigid and staring while he is drawn up on this little piece of wire 800 feet above the canyon floor, is carried across to the ledge, steps off and walks away without looking back. Such is the spirit of Boulder Dam.

More than a hundred men have been killed building this dam. It's sort of like aviation; some die, and others keep right on working, putting a big wad of concrete across one of the world's muddiest rivers.

Out West there's an old gag about the Colorado that "It's too thick to drink and too thin to plow." So they make electricity out of it.

—April 9, 1935

THIRST IN THE DESERT

TACNA, Ariz.—Thirty miles south of Tacna, almost to the Mexican border, is a place called Tinajas Altas, which means "High Tanks." It is a series of natural basins, one above the other, on a desert hillside. They catch and hold rain water. It was a favorite desert watering place in the early days.

On the slope above Tinajas Altas are countless graves of men. You can identify only a few now but when Ike Proebstal first came here 33 years ago he and his brother counted 160 graves one day. Every one was of a man who had died from thirst. Men who had groped across the deathly hot desert, hoped their last hope on finding water at Tinajas Altas and not finding it, died.

Proebstal says the tale is that a Mexican bandit named Blanco operated there in the '49 gold rush days. He would sneak across the border and drain the tanks. Then when the thirsting gold seekers, California-bound, died their choking deaths, he would rob them.

Ike Proebstal knows about men who die of thirst. For 33 years he has been a prospector and a mining man among these snaky sands and bare mountains, and he has saved many a man from death.

A fellow down the road said to me, "When Ike Proebstal tells you anything about this country you can bank on it being true." Proebstal is truly an unusual man. In the first place, he's one of the handsomest humans I ever laid eyes on. He carries his 60-odd years like a lord. He has a little Continental goatee, and I'll bet there's isn't a man in Berlin who would so grace a silk hat and opera coat.

He was born in Oregon, studied mining engineering, and then lit out. Was in the South African mines for years, spent a year on the Australian desert, four years in Hawaii, a year in China and Japan. What strange careers these desert spaces gather into their folds! Ike Proebstal has been rich and he has been poor. Today he lives in a one-room shack, but he's not desert rat.

"I wish my brother were still alive to talk with you," he said. "He had a real reputation for finding missing men. But I've saved quite a few, too. The first 15 years we were here, my brother and I rescued at least two people a year, I guess.

"You know, a man dying from thirst always takes off all his clothes. I don't know why, but they do it every time.

"I remember one fellow I rescued years ago. A man rode into my prospecting camp late in the afternoon. He was more dead than alive, and his horse was, too. He said he had left his partner under a bush about five miles away.

"I started right out. I ran almost all the way, for I knew I could just barely make it by sundown. I knew that if I didn't get there before dark I'd never find him, for he'd get up at dusk and start traveling. They always do it.

"Well, I found him. He was lying there on the sand, naked as a baby. A few feet away was a tripod made of stout steel tubing about two feet long, with a kettle hanging on it. I kicked the tripod down and stood there and called to the fellow.

"I said 'I've got some water for you, come and get it.' The fellow raised up. His face was black as coal, and his tongue was swollen and sticking out of his mouth two inches. He jumped up and ran at me and tried to take the water from me.

"But I handled him all right. I'd brought a canteen of water and a whiskey glass. I gave him just one small glass of water. Then I made him put his clothes on, and told him if he'd follow me I'd give him a drink every 150 yards.

"The boys back at the camp had built bonfires so I could find my way back. When we got about half way I asked the fellow how he was feeling, and he said fine, that he was sweating. So I said, 'all right, then you can drink all you want now.'

"He told me later that he was crazy and yet he wasn't crazy. He said he saw me standing over those steel bars, and he knew why I was doing it. He said if it hadn't been for those bars he would have killed be to get at the water quicker."

Do you know that on a blistering hot summer day in the Arizona desert a man lives only three or four hours after the thirst craze hits him? That's what Ike Proebstal says.

Ike almost got it once. He tried too long a hike between water holes, and the thirst craze set in. If he hadn't knowns the ways of the desert he'd be a dead one now.

"But there isn't much sense of dying of thirst nowadays," he says. "For instance, my wife and I are going on a little prospecting trip tomorrow. We'll take plenty of water in the car, and we'll leave word here where we're going, and if we're not back by 10 o'clock tomorrow night they'll start looking for us.

"I don't know what it is about the desert. It's a God forsaken place. But it gets in your blood. I've lived all over the world, but I haven't been away from here now for 23 years. I couldn't live anywhere else."

– January 6, 1937

KEG OF NAILS ON THE AJO ROAD

PHOENIX, Ariz.—Just a few Southwest odds and ends. Two for a nickel or four for a dime, Take 'em or leave 'em.

One night here in Phoenix a well-dressed drunk came in and ordered a glass of beer. He sat down at the counter, fingered his glass, looked slowly around, surveying the people, and then made his pronouncement:

"The trouble with Anthony Adverse is that it's lacking in first and second class."

Nobody said anything at first but finally the bartender said, "First and second class what?"

"Just what I said," the drunk answered. "First and second class." That's all they ever got out of him.

One morning I got up early and drove 45 miles over a gravel road from Gila Bend to Ajo, to see a man. The man wasn't there. I drove back.

On the way back I met a big truck with a funny contraption on the back end. I asked the hitch-hiker who was with me what it was. He didn't know. Just as we got back to Gila Bend a rear tire started going flat. I shot into a garage and had it changed. We pulled out a bent nail three inches long.

Then the garageman got to telling me about nails on the Ajo road. About three years ago, he said, a supply truck was going to Ajo and a keg of roofing nails broke open. The driver didn't know it and he scattered nails from Gila Bend to Ajo.

The garageman said he had a call to go down and fix a fellow's tires, and when he got there all four tires were flat. They pulled 26 nails out of just one tire.

Then they sent to Phoenix for "the magnet." That's the funny truck I had seen on the road. There are still so many nails spilled on this highway that they get the magnet down twice a year to go over it. It gets a bushel of nails every trip.

Speaking of roads, there's one in America that I have a peculiar attachment for. It's the old corduroy road across the California desert west of Yuma. I drove over it 10 years ago. It ran for some ten miles across the only piece of absolutely bare, shifting, drifting, fine-sand desert in America.

What is generally called desert in the Southwest is not absolutely bare. It is usually rocky, and has a prettty full growth of cactus or sage, plus several kinds of little dry bushes and weeds. But this "American Sahara" west of Yuma is barren and it piles in beautiful rippled dunes, and it swirls and it drifts.

The old corduroy road across it was just wide enough for one car. Every quarter of a mile or so there would be a "pullout," for cars to pass. Ten years ago they said a solid road could never be built across this shifting sand.

It gave me a thrill and made me feel like a pioneer, to drive over that road then. But it gives me just as big a thrill to speed over the fine paved highway and see the sad, black remains of that old road lying out there, half-covered with sand, upended, rotting, and to say to people, "I actually drove over that road."

I've noticed this—you can talk to a farmer or a cattleman or a desert man all day long and he'll talk freely and answer the most personal questions, but he'll never ask your name or your business or where you're from.

And I've also noticed this—that all supposedly superb climates are overrated.

In Southern California, for instance, you have about four hours of delightful summer weather around midday. You shed your vest about 9 a.m. and your coat at 11. But by 2 you have your coat back on, by 4 you're looking for your vest; by 6 you need your topcoat and all night you're in agony from the damp, boring cold. Getting up of a morning is torture.

California, here I go—back to where it's 10 above zero and I'll be cursing myself for having left California.

One thing about the Southwest, from Texas on—they do observe traffic signals. A pedestrian in Phoenix would no more think of walking against the lights than the chief of police would think of driving across against the lights.

Pedestrians stand and wait for the green light, even if there isn't a car in sight. It gives you a feeling of great security. I wish people in the East weren't too smart to try it.

The funniest thing I've seen in the Southwest—some 30 miles east of Yuma, right out there where there's nothing as far as you can see but sand and 2500 miles from the Atlantic Ocean, is a huge signboard advertising the Hotel Edison in New York City.

— January 8, 1937

BOOM-TOWN'S BABY IS 73

WINNEMUCCA, Nev.—This afternoon I went out to the edge of town to see an old "desert rat" prospector. When I got there he said he wasn't a "desert rat."

"I've got a good education," he said "and all the money I need. I've got good clothes hanging in that closet, and I could put them on and go downtown and nobody would know me."

W. H. Harris is 73 now. His face is long and sensitive, and very wrinkled. He is gray, and his heart bothers him.

He wears striped overalls and shaves with an electric razor. He rolls brown-paper cigarets, folds the end, and smokes them without licking them. He talks in a quiet, melancholy voice, and his theme is one of despair.

He was born in Virginia City, Nev., when that town was the hottest boom camp the U. S. has ever had. He has spent his lifetime between the machine shops of San Francisco and the bare sage hills of Nevada.

He prefers the hills. But he says every gold mine he ever found has brought him trouble. Lawsuits come like rain, and greedy schemers move in on you. He won't look for any more mines, altho he would like to be back in the hills. He is unhappy. He doesn't know what to do.

Four years ago he moved in from the desert, after 20 years out there in a cabin beside his mine. He moved in because his family got sick of the desert. He says it was the worst move he ever made. He doesn't like town.

He owns two big homes in Alameda, Calif. His wife and son live there, and want him to come down, but he doesn't think that would work either. No place to walk.

He says nobody here he can talk to. He used to read a lot, but lately he can't get interested in anything he reads.

He has a completely equipped machine shop, with intricate lathes and planes and all sorts of tools. He does beautiful cabinet work. But the shop is a junk heap now; he can't get interested in making anything.

He sees greed all around him, and he can't understand it. He gave a banker acquaintance a little piece of gold-streaked quartz, just as a memento for a watch fob. The banker had it pounded into dust and assayed, to see how much gold was in it.

There was a thing in the early days of mining in Nevada called the "Spirit of the Comstock." It meant that whatever you had, you shared with somebody else. Everybody had so much it didn't make any difference anyhow.

The "Spirit of the Comstock" is mostly gone now, but it does live on in Billy Harris.

He has two cabins on the edge of town. Not elaborate, but good-sized cabins, sitting there in the alkali dust. He lets one poor family live in the front half of one, while he stays in the back bedroom and kitchen. And another family, on relief, lives in the other cabin. They pay no rent. He's good for a touch any time, altho he doesn't look as tho he had a dime.

Ten years ago Harris invented a machine known as a "dry washer." It's a washing-machine-like affair; you turn a crank, and a paddle inside makes a great whirring noise. Its purpose is to capture fine gold dust from gravel, instead of using a pan or rocker box. It gets dust that is so fine it would float away on the water of a gold pan.

He could have made a fortune off these "dry washers." He has letters about them from nearly every country on the globe. He could license a manufacturer, and the royalties would be handsome. But he lets a friend in California build and sell them without fee, and he signed away the royalty rights to a big company which makes them in the Philippines. He didn't want to be bothered.

He has made about 250 of them himself in the past 10 years. They're worth about $200 apiece. But most of his have gone to poor prospector friends. He didn't charge anything for them. He just made one whenever he felt like it. He isn't even interested in making them any more.

He doesn't care for glory, or more money, or what people think of him. He has reached the almost Utopian stage of simplicity, selflessness and indifference. And yet he is miserable. Life seems just to have withered away from him.

In his shed is a big Chrysler "chuck wagon," fully equipped for living and prospecting in the desert. The license tags say "1935," and the engine hasn't been started for two years. The door handles are all rusted. Dust from the passing parade of traffic is settled thickly upon it.

— November 19, 1937

TRAGEDY AND RICHES TRAILED BONANZA KINGS

VIRGINIA CITY, Nev.—I have been reading books to "prep" myself on the history of the greatest gold and silver camp the U. S. has ever known—Virginia City. The books were built around the careers of the great bonanza kings of the Comstock Lode.

The first king was Henry "Old Pancake" Comstock. He didn't make the find himself. His loud voice scared the real finders into giving him a share, and naming it after him. (He never knew he was king till after it was over. He was out of Virginia City within a year after the strike.) Of those four men who first staked the Comstock, one died in poverty, one died in an asylum, one fell off a horse while drunk and was killed, and one committed suicide. The suicide was "Old Pancake" Comstock.

The second king was William Sharon. He was small, bald, foppish. But with the Bank of California behind him he grabbed the Comstock and for 10 years ruled it with a monopolisitic ruthlessness that is historic. When he lost the throttle he went on to the U.S. Senate and remained a millionaire.

The third king was not one man but a set of four, working together. They rose from muckers and saloonkeepers to make fortunes of two hundred millions. Their names were John W. Mackay (father of Clarence Mackay), James G. Fair (whose daughters married Vanderbilts and Oelrichs), James C. Flood and William S. O'Brien.

They were the greatest kings of the Comstock, and they worked the famous lode until it began to play out in 1878. They founded fortunes which endure today.

The fourth king took over when that foursome stepped out. His name was Adolph Sutro, and to me he is the noblest figure of the Comstock, because he fought so long and so tenaciously on the side of a mere dream. The story is too long to tell. But his victory was almost too late, and he abdicated after two years.

And the fifth king—a modern king—occupies the previous throne today. It isn't the throne it used to be. The king isn't the kind they used to have. He sits on top of the Comstock Lode, and tho millions still lie beneath him he may never get them.

I went to call on him. His name is James Leonard. He is a gracious, gentle-voiced man of late middle age. He is the head of the company that controls the Comstock Lode today.

They own most of the ground that covers the great vein. They own the famous seven-mile Sutro tunnel which bores 2000 feet beneath Virginia City and drains the steaming waters and foul air of the mines. They own the important water works system, which brings water from the Sierras. And they are operating mines and mills today.

If the Comstock should ever come back—I mean come back as it was in the '60s and '70s—James Leonard would be a Midas. And he expects it to come back.

James Leonard has lived in Virginia City for nearly 40 years. He came out from New York with his father when Sutro, the last king, was abdicating. The elder Leonard started buying in and today the control is tight.

James Leonard lives in a big white house one block above the main street. The ceilings are 20 feet high. The company offices are on the first floor. Leonard sits at a big old desk, and there is one girl secretary in the place.

There is sentiment and a tenderness for romance in Leonard's character. He rode around with me for hours, pointing out things. He took me to the gulch where the first strike was made. We stood in the doorway where Mark Twain used to stand and spit.

He showed me the great porched-all-around mansions of the old mine superintendents. We took a glance at the famos copper chandelier in the Crystal Bar, hanging there since 1864. He showed me Piper's Opera House, where Edwin Booth and Nat Goodwin and Patti and Modjeska came to entertain the newly rich.

"There is romance in every brick of this old town." he said "Writers come here and ridicule us. But some day Virginia will come back."

And it wouldn't surprise me if it did. Because geologists say the Comstock is a true fissure vein, which means the metals extends down and down, nobody knows how far.

They've never mined the Comstock below 2000 feet, because that is the level of the Sutro drainage tunnel. To go below that at present would be impractical. There must be deeper drainage, and ventilation, and refrigeration of the hellishly hot depths. It would take a terrific amount of money.

But as machinery advances, and men start to plunge again with their money, it doesn't seem impossible that another $700,000,000 might come boiling up from the lower regions of the Comstock Lode.

Of course you mustn't buy any stock on my say-so. For there is no indication right now that any such invasion of the Comstock will be made in our time. But people think it's still rich down there, and as long as there's a mucker or a gambler or a metal visionary left in Nevada you never can tell what might happen.

— November 27, 1937

OLD-TIMERS RECALL FABULOUS MEMORIES

VIRGINIA CITY, Nev.—There's an old whitish house on a sort of ledge in the hillside on the upper edge of Virginia City.

There is a white fence around it, and a gate with an old-fashioned latch. An oldish man in overalls comes out and shakes your hand. He is small and a little stooped.

He is Jimmy Stoddard. He is the Comstock's only living bridge between the far past and the present. He has been on the Comstock for 75 years.

"I guess you go back further than anybody else in Virginia City, don't you?" I asked. Of course people had told me that; that's the reason I went to see him.

"I think you called the turn on that one, son," he said. "I think you called that one right. I guess I'm the oldest, all right."

Jimmy Stoddard arrived here with his parents from New York in 1864. He was 9 then. His parents lie buried over on the hill. You can see the graveyard from his house.

He went to work in the bowels of the Comstock when he was 13, and there he worked until he was 71. Fifty-eight years in the mines, right beneath Virginia City. Jimmy Stoddard is 84 now, but he still goes out in the hills and prospects around.

He is a truthful man, and admits he doesn't remember awfully much about the early days. He doesn't recall that he ever saw Mark Twain; he does remember seeing many a man hanging from the beams of the shaft houses in the old days; he says he ran the cage that brought Gen. U.S. Grant up from the mines on his visit here in '78; he says that in the boom days miners on their way to work would slip an order for stock under the bank door, and when they came out of the earth that evening they'd be $500 richer, just by speculation; and they they'd go to San Francisco and spend it all. He was one of them.

His memory is clear but not spectacular. Seventy-five years is a long time to recall details and keep things straight in your head.

But not all the old-timers remember as unspectacularly as Jimmy Stoddard. The most remarkable remembering is done by those who tell you all about Mark Twain. It's truly amazing how sharp their recollections are.

One old fellow told me that altho Twain is known as a humorist nobody around Virginia City ever saw him smile. This old man remembers him well, even refers to him as "Sam."

He says Twain used to stand all the time in the doorway of The Enterprise Bulding and spit tobacco juice onto the steps of the adjoining doctor's office, which happened to belong to this old man's uncle.

So this old man (just a boy then, of course) called his uncle's attention to it, and the uncle put up a sign not to spit there. So after that Twain stood in the doorway and instead of spitting on the steps he spit on the new sign.

I thought that was a grand little story, and I had a sort of thrill from talking with a man who had actually known Mark Twain in those far days when they called him "Sam."

Before parting, I asked the old man his age, and he told me. When I got home I figured back on the dates—and discovered that this old man wasn't even born till a year after Mark Twain left Virginia City forever. That's the kind of memory I admire.

Today not a single descendant of the Comstock's great bonanza kings has any financial holdings in the remnants of the Comstock. They have taken other courses.

They tell you around here that the first-generation descendants are still interested in Virginia City sentimentally. Some of them come here occasionally to talk and look over old spots.

Clarence Mackay, of Postal Telegraph, whose father was the king of kings of the Comstock, comes back every few years. He always goes into the Catholic Church and says a prayer in memory of his parents.

But the second generation, they say, has no interest in Virginia City. In fact, some of them are quite, quite ashamed of the roughness of their grandfathers.

I was told of one incident that happened not long ago. The grandson of one of the bonanza kings showed up with his bride. A pleased old-timer volunteered to show them around.

So he steered the couple out past the edge of town, up a little gulch a hundred yards or so, and then stopped and said, with an emotion which was filling him:

"Right there is the spot where your grandfather staked his first claim."

And the rich grandson said, "Isn't the view gorgeous from here?"

The old-timer thought he hadn't been heard. So he said again: "There, right in front of you, is the very ground where your grandfather made his great strike."

And the rich grandson said, "Aren't the clouds over there magnificent?"

And the old-timer replied, with what seems to me exactly the proper answer, "Well, you can go straight to hell."

And he turned and went back down the gulch, leaving them there.

ERNIE LAMENTS SINLESS LIFE

LAS VEGAS, Nev.—Since I am an extremely frail child, subject to the slightest draft or change of season, I suppose it is only natural that I should be, once again, down with the miseries.

It is my impression that I have pneumonia. My traveling partner calls it flu. The hotel maid refers to it as the grippe. The doctor says it is just a common house cold.

At any rate I am incapacitated, and there seems nothing to do but lie here for a few days and look back upon my sins. Yet even that privilege is denied me.

For my life has been one of continuous purity, righteousness and good deeds. There are no sins to look back upon. I am very unhappy.

Why could I not have sinned a little in my lifetime? If I come out of this alive, I shall leave no cactus unturned until I have gathered a list of good black sins. I don't intend to be caught like this again.

With my last few breaths I will try to give you an item or two. The first is a rather incomplete one about the late Arthur Brisbane's ranch.

The great columnist owned a ranch on the Mojave Desert in south central California, a few miles from the little town of Victorville. A fellow in Los Angeles told me that during the latter years of his life Brisbane spent more than half his time out here.

Well, we drove several miles beyond Victorville and didn't see any ranch, so I thought I'd better inquire. We came to a little settlement and pulled up in front of a garage, where two men were working on a car.

One of them wiped his hands and came out, and I said: "Can you tell me where the Brisbane ranch is?"

He said, "Who?"

I said, "Arthur Brisbane's ranch."

He looked puzzled, and then went back to the man under the car and said: "Arthur Brisbane. Do you know him?"

The other man got out from under the car, wiped his hands, and said: "Arthur Brisbane? Yes, it's six miles on up the highway, on the right-hand side."

The first fellow still looked prodigiously puzzled.

Six miles down the road we did pass a ranch house, which I can only assume was Brisbane's. Somehow I didn't have the nerve to drive in and ask questions. The place sat about a quarter-mile off the highway, and looked more like a bunch of homesteaders' buildings than a multi-millionaire's retreat.

And why Brisbane ever picked that spot I can't figure out. The desert there seems to me very third-class. It isn't pretty; there is no magnificent long view; the wind just seems to blow mournfully over dull flatness.

Personally I'm a sort of desert lover, and I can see more variety of scenery and more inspiring views on the desert than almost anywhere else. But the Mojave around Brisbane's ranch gives me a feeling of a vacant lot, just stretched out as far as you can see.

There is a strange custom on the Mojave Desert. It is glass-coloring.

It seems that if you leave a piece of glass out in the sun a few years, it will turn blue, amber, or purple. The desert sun has a violet-ray effect.

Nearly every desert dweller has a stack of candlesticks, ash trays, doorknobs, bottles and dishes lying out on the ground, coloring.

They bring good prices. One fellow said he turned down $5 for an ashtray. One woman sells broken-off bottle tops for 50 cents apiece. One house where we stopped had a glass doorknob that had been coloring for 50 years.

I haven't told you about my rocks. At one house where we stopped, the man got out his hammer and broke off half a dozen pieces of various desert rocks, and made me put them in the car.

I don't know why it is, but people are always giving me rocks. I must look rock-conscious. I've got samples of rock all the way from Guatemala to the Bering Sea. People give me rocks and I always intend to throw them away around the next bend, but I never do.

In my trunk at home I'll bet there's 50 pounds of rock. That's one reason I've never made a will. If the executors found my trunkful of rocks they'd tell the judge I was crazy and the will would be thrown out.

A sort of hysterical peak in my rock-gathering career was reached the other day when a fellow sent me, thru the mail, a sack of ground-up rock. He said I should eat it, and it would cure me of leprosy.

I haven't got leprosy, but I wonder what three tablespoons of ground rock would do for the common house cold? Unfortunately I shall never know.

—March 30, 1938

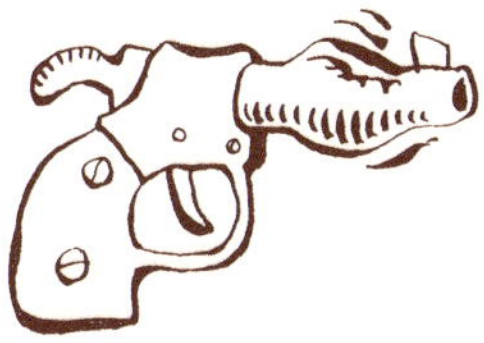

ANOTHER BILLY THE KID TALL TALE

OLD MESILLA, N.M.—George Griggs sat at the fireplace in his rocking chair and said: "Reach up to that third gun on the wire there."

"This one?" I asked. He nodded.

It was a small pistol with a short barrel, and the barrel was split open on top, about an inch back from the nose.

"How did that happen?" I asked.

"Well, there was a Jew that kept trying to pick a fight with Billy the Kid in a saloon. Billy the Kid was tough, but he liked Jews, and didn't want to hurt this fellow, so he just kept telling him to go away. But the Jew was in a bad mood, and he was bound to pick a fight. Finally the Kid gave him a shove and told him to get out of there, and then the Jew started to pull his gun.

"Well, Billy pulled quick and fired. He didn't want to hurt the fellow. So he fired right into the muzzle of his gun, in order to stop his bullet.

"That split there, that's where the Kid's bullet going in met the Jew's bullet coming out. It just split the barrel wide open." George Griggs got up and fumbled on the mantel. "Here are the bullets," he said. "See how they're all twisted up."

I looked a long time at the pistol's split barrel. And at the deformed bullets, which were too big to go in either the split or the muzzle, and then at George Griggs.

"Do you believe that?" I said.

He answered: "Well, I don't know much about guns. I'm not really much interested in guns. I'm interested mostly in Mexican blankets and pottery. I don't know whether to believe it or not. I guess it's true."

This "Billy the Kid Museum" is famous all over the Southwest. It isn't like a museum at all. It's just a hodgepode of stuff in an old adobe house.

Mesilla is an old, old town. It is as if you were dreaming of old Mexico. The streets are of dust. The buildings are of red-brown adobe. Flat. Colorless.

The wind whirls the sand mercilessly, and you can hardly walk against it. Only the sand seems alive. There is little other movement in old Mesilla.

George Griggs was born here. He has traveled far; was educated highly. But he has been back in Mesilla for a long time now. He lives alone amidst his collection and he fits into it.

He is stall and thin and stooped, and his pants are much too long. A

scraggly beard covers his long, intellectual face, and he sports a huge bow tie. He is no longer young. He speaks in a loud, confidential whisper.

He makes a bare living out of this museum. He charges the tourists a quarter.

But George Griggs is independent, and a little temperamental. If the wind is blowing, or he isn't in the mood, he won't go to the door when tourists knock.

I spent three hours with him and I was there two hours before I could get him to talk about Billy the Kid or show me any of his stuff.

The paramount interest in George Griggs' life today is whether the Gadsen Purchase of 1853 put the line eight miles north of El Paso or 48 miles north.

It is not my privilege to be able to state which side of the argument Mr. Griggs is on. He has all kinds of documents to prove his point, provided you know the point. He has documents to prove that the National Geographic Magazine is either a liar or a champion of his belief, one or the other. Showing off these documents is Mr. Griggs' favorite pastime.

It disgusts George Griggs the way tourists get him all mixed up. Some think he was a pal of Billy the Kid. Some think he is the man who killed Billy the Kid. And some, not so well up on their bad-man history, think he's Billy the Kid himself.

As a matter of fact, Griggs only saw Billy the Kid once. Griggs was a little boy, and had been sent to the saloon for a bucket of beer. The saloon, incidentally, was in this very room where the Kid's guns now hang on baling wire over the mantel.

Little George Griggs went in the door, and recognized one of the men in the saloon as the famous killer and little George Griggs turned and ran as fast as he could go.

Griggs wants to sell his museum and spend the rest of his days in California. He is getting old, and this Billy the Kid stuff just attracts fool tourists like me who aren't interested in the Gadsden Purchase. He'll sell the whole batch for $10,000.

He has had some good offers, but he says: "Whenever I get an offer the women's clubs and historical societies start writing in and saying, "Oh, Mr. Griggs, you ought to be more patriotic than that. You ought to give your stuff to our society."

– April 11, 1938

RIDDLE OF CHACO CANYON

CHACO CANYON, N. M.–We are in a valley in northwestern New Mexico. Our valley is 10 miles long and a mile wide. On each side the canyon rim rises abruptly to the mesa top a hundred feet up.

Once upon a time, 10,000 people lived in this small valley. That was nearly a thousand years ago. They lived in apartment houses, and one of them was so big it was never equalled in size anywhere in the world until 40 years ago.

You can come here today and see, still more than half standing, this amazing apartment house of our early Indians.

Chaco Canyon is a national monument. If you are untraveled in the West, you might as well get this national monument thing straightened out right now.

I used to think a national monument was a big statue or marker put up to honor something. But it isn't. It's a large tract of land set aside by the Government because of its historic or scenic value. It is actually a No. 2 national park.

The Southwest is full of national monuments. Some are scenic phenomena, such as the natural bridges, volcanic craters, bad lands and painted deserts. Others contain the remnants of the civilization that once existed here.

Chaco Canyon is one of these. Indians lived and farmed and built in this 10-mile valley for some 200 to 300 years. They started building here around the year 900. Their last building was about 1130.

This valley at that time must have been very fertile. A flowing river ran thru it, whereas today there is only a dry wash: They cut trees on the mesa tops that were two feet across. Today anything bigger than a sage brush clump makes your eyes stick out.

At that time things were fresh and green and pleasant. Today all is dry and harsh; the wind blows unmercifully, the sand whips thru the air, and on the mesa top you can scream and not be heard six inches away above the wind.

In this 10-mile canyon, 18 important ruins have been discovered. There are undoubtedly more to be found, when they get around to it.

Pueblo Bonito is the one tourists are most likely to see if they come here. It is an apartment house in a D-shape. The flat side of the D probably was low, but the curved part ran up to five stories high. The building covers three acres and had about 800 rooms.

It is built of the flat stones found lying on the ground in these parts. There must have been billions of stones in this vast pueblo. The Indian women did the masonry work.

The earliest construction was poor. Then a hundred years or so later, they reached a very commendable state of masonry work. And then the later buildings were poor again. Why was that? I'll bite. Why?

You can wander thru this old ruin, and put your hands up and feel of logs and even reeds that have been right there in the ceiling for 1000 years. It is misleading merely to say the wood is well-preserved. It is, in fact, as good as if it were cut 20 years ago.

The doors to all the rooms are very low—about two feet high. Which might indicate they were little people. Yet the ceilings are so high a seven-footer could stand upright.

Many of the doors from one room to another, instead of being in the side-wall, go thru the corner of the room.

The pueblo was built over to the edge of the canyon bottom, only a few feet from the perpendicular rock wall that is the canyon side. Right behind the pueblo a gigantic slab of rock has split off. It is 100 feet high and must be 75 feet wide.

Today they call it Threatening Rock. It was undoubtedly split even at the time the Indians lived here. Maybe it scared them away, who knows? Scientists are watching it now, and measuring its movement. Some day it may come crashing down.

Chaco Canyon Monument is not a place for the vast stream of tourists. Only those who are really interested come here. You're on unpaved road for 60 miles in each direction, and it is a townless, forbidding country. There were 90 visitors last month.

I think I shan't go see any more Indian ruins. For they are exasperating. They raise a question, and leave it unanswered.

At Mesa Verde, the Basket-Makers disappeared. Nobody knows why or where. And here at Cacho Canyon, the two great questions are, "Where did they come from? Where did they go?" You ask with tiredness and resignation, for there is no answer. Nobody knows.

Today there is some modern population in the canyon. A caretaker and summer Park Ranger. A CCC camp of Navajo boys. A trading post where you can buy groceries. And, in August, archeological students from the University of New Mexico, who come here and live in Indian "hogans" and dig among the ruins.

The Government has plans for building a road up to the mesa top, and erecting a modern lodge up there. It will take several years.

When that is done, tourists can come, and sit on the mesa rim by the hour, and stare down at the amazingly intricate and vast apartment where once 1200 human beings lived and worked and loved and disappeared. Just as we ourselves will do. And what of it?

—July 21, 1939

ERNIE SITS ON FOUR STATES IN ONE SITTING

FOUR CORNERS, U.S.A.—I've been holding my breath for years for fear Mrs. Roosevelt would beat me to this spot. But as far as I know, I made it first.

This is the only place in America where four states come together. And please, please don't any of you readers write in and say "What of it?", for I don't know any answer.

Way off here in the mountainous desert, at a tiny mathematical pin-point, the states of Colorado, Utah, Arizona and New Mexico all touch each other.

There's nothing out here except a concrete post, and two swallows that keep flying around. Nobody but some screwball like me would think of coming out here to write about it.

This spot is isolated. We drove out here in the car. But, if any of you should decide to follow our example and honor Four Corners with a visit, I'd suggest you bring a saddle. Also a shovel and water and great capacity for gazing at nothingness.

You get here by driving 30 miles west from Shiprock, N.M., on a dirt road. At 30 miles you turn right, onto a couple of tracks. You follow these tracks another eight miles.

It takes you three-quarters of an hour to go the last eight miles. It's uphill, and full of rocks and drifted sand. You may have to stop and boil, as we did. If the wind has been blowing too much sand lately, you may even get stuck.

When you finally get here, you'll find a concrete post about two feet high, put up by the Government. On top of it is set a bronze plate, not quite at big as a saucer. Stamped on this plate are two little lines, about an inch long, crossing in the middle. Those are the boundary lines between the four states.

We got kind of silly when we got here. First thing, I had to sit on top of the post, which made my rather scant bottom repose in four states simultaneously. I don't care how big your bottom is, you can't do better than that.

After that, I leaned over the monument, and had my picture taken with one foot in Utah and one in Colorado, a hand in New Mexico and one in Arizona. Didn't even feel ridiculous while I did it, either.

Then we got out our sandwiches, and I sat on the post eating in one-twelfth of America all at once. When we finished I threw a handful of banana peels and pieces of bread up in the air, and they fell in four states at once, desecrating them with refuse. The dirtiest tourist in the land can't out-desecrate me.

The friend who was with me set about collecting rocks for his three children back home. It seems his children are rock lovers, and he's always carrying rocks home.

He picked up several rocks from each state for each child. He wrote down on a piece of paper what state they were from. But he didn't write on the rocks.

If he can tell one rock from another when he gets home, I'll buy him a whole trainload of quartz. Quartz with streaks of gold in it, too.

For 30 feet around the marker post there are circles on that ground, where tourists have driven around and around. Of course I had to do it, too.

So my friend timed me, and it took just 10 seconds to circle the post, cutting the wheels as short as they would go. That gave me two and a half seconds in each of the four states. A colossal achievement, my friends, a colossal achievement!

Very few people ever get to Four Corners. At Shiprock, they say that one car a week would be stretching it.

For one thing, most people never heard of it. For another, those last eight miles are just an old Navajo wagon trail, and aren't even on the road maps.

It is not especially nice right here at Four Corners. The monument is set in the center of a little plateau, a block or so square. From there the land falls away, or rises, into the vast, rolling, desolate, windy country that is this part of the world. The sight is majestic in all directions. But it is not gentle.

Not 100 yards from the marker post are the crude stone walls of a crumbled building. There is no floor, no roof, no doors. We were told that somebody tried to start a tourist hotel here. But later we learned it was merely a trading post, which went broke.

Inside it now is nothing but a pile of rocks and an old shoe. There is evidence that the wandering flocks of Navajo sheep take refuge in it occasionally.

The idea of building a hotel out here sort of intrigued me—until I got here. But I am now of the opinion that I'd think a long time before trying to entice the gay public out to Four Corners. I doubt I could stay here myself long enough to get the foundation built.

I couldn't help but compare today's little luncheon with the day we ate right on the Equator, up there 10,000 feet in the windy vastness of the Andes of South America.

And except that our lunch wasn't as good today, there was almost no difference at all.

– July 22, 1939

THE INDIANS JUST STARED

TEEC NOS PAS, Ariz.—This column is an account of 15 minutes in Teec Nos Pas.

Teec Nos Pas is an Indian trading post. There are scores of them scattered about the vast Navajo reservation. Most of them are exorbitantly isolated.

This country is full of vast desolation. You drive and you look, and you say, "Lord, what waste! This is utter emptiness. How does anybody make a living?"

The road becomes a mere trail. You jounce over solid sheets of outcropping rock. Thousands of acres of flat solid rock, like fields of concrete. The end of nowhere.

You come around a rough little hill, and there in the valley is Teec Nos Pas. Just the store and a few outbuildings, that's all. A store in the desert.

Loafing Indians lay on the porch, lounged against store walls. Indian ponies, saddled and blanketed, were tied here and there. The Indians wore red bands around their heads.

We stopped and walked toward the store. One of two white men lounging on the porch got up and went in ahead of us. All the loafing Indian eyes drilled us coldly.

In the West, there is a friendly greeting between strangers. But not at Teec Nos Pas. The unfriendly store, the sinister eye, is the greeting at Teec Nos Pas.

The store was old and dirty inside. Lying on the floor, flat on his back, was an old Indian. Just lying there, doing nothing, talking to nobody, looking at nothing. Nobody anywhere doing anything, except staring.

We wanted to buy something, to break the ice. "I'll have a Coca-Cola," said my friend. "No cold drinks here," said the white trader.

There was no friendliness in that store. Only a belligerent waiting to see who you were and what the hell brought you here. My friend bought a sack of Bull Durham.

"Can you tell me anything about that old building up at Four Corners?" I asked.

The trader leaned one elbow against the high candy case. He pulled at his cigaret, held his head back, blew high. And then he said, with utter finality:

"Don't know anything about it."

I knew better, so I waited awhile, and then said, "Never even heard of it, huh?"

Then I waited a bit and said, "You been out here long?" And after awhile the trader said, "Yes, quite a while." And then he said:

"I thought you were tourists. I hoped you were tourists and gonna look at a rug."

We kind of laughed to ease the tension, and I said, "Well, how can you tell we're not tourists? Do we look too poor to buy a rug?"

The trader said no, that wasn't it.

One by one the porch-sitting Indians were drifting in, and standing around. Not an expression of any kind was on their faces. They stood and stared, like so many animal eyes around a campfire.

There was no conversation except that between the trader and me, and it was toilsome and unwelcome conversation to us both. I tried again:

"I hear somebody tried to start a hotel. That old building up there."

The trader said "No, it wasn't a hotel. It was a trading post."

"I'd heard it was a hotel," I said.

"That's the Indian agent out there on the porch. He can tell you what you want to know."

After a bit the agent drifted in. He did not speak. He sat on the high counter across the store, and studied the old Army shoes my friend wore. Waiting us out. Our move.

"How long has it been since you sold a rug to a tourist?" I asked the trader.

He blew a disdainful answer of smoke thru his nose. "God, I don't know. Tourists never come here. Nobody ever comes here."

The Indian agent continued his study. The Indians watched to see if my friend could actually roll a cigaret. He could. Their expression did not change.

The old Indian on the floor never moved. The heat was oppressive, and the needles in the air grew sharper. My friend and I sensed each other's wishes without looking.

"Well, I reckon we better shove along," I said.

"I reckon we better," my friend replied.

Stares propelled us out the door. The rocky road away from Teec Nos Pas felt like a ribbon of velvet. The desert felt clean and safe and pure.

– July 24, 1939

HE LOVES AND FEARS THE RIVER

MEXICAN HAT, Utah—In each of these little settlements down thru the deserts of the Navajo country one white family stands out.

In some cases they wouldn't have to stand very far, because there is only one white family. But, without exception, we find them to be unusual people.

Each of these settlements comes to be known as much by the name of the family as by its real name. And so it is that "The Nevills" is practically synonymous with Mexican Hat.

You probably have heard of the Nevills, altho you may not remember it. For it was Norman Nevills who kept the wire services and newspapers in hot water for more than a month last summer with his expedition down the Colorado River.

The party was 42 days making the 660 miles from Green River, Utah, to Boulder Dam. For days and weeks they were supposedly "lost" and even dead. But they came thru, and if you've ever shot a rapids with Norman Nevills you'll understand why they came thru.

It is about Norman Nevills that I'm writing today. There are two families of Nevills here. Norman and his wife and little girl in one house. And his parents in another.

The elder Nevills was a California oil engineer. He came to this majestically bare country in 1920 as an oil man. He has been here ever since. Today he is in very poor health, and he says that even to say a few words exhausts him.

Norman and his mother run the Indian trading post, and the tasteful lodge where they put up those wayfarers from far away who travel this part of the desert. To Norman, those things are sidelines. The river is his main life.

Norman came here in 1925, to monkey in the oil business with his father. He is a college graduate from California, and had studied engineering. They had a lot of money at one time.

But they shot in all in oil, and didn't get it back. Norman is glad, now, for otherwise he might never has stayed so long, and today he loves it here above any other place in the world. He is, I would say, not much over 30.

In the daytime he wears old overalls and a shirt with the sleeves torn out. In the evening he changes to a spic summer sports outfit.

He speaks some Navajo and dickers patiently with the Indians who bring in rugs to trade for supplies. His mother says Norman offers the Indians too little. Norman says his mother offers them too much. But the Indians must like it, for they're always hanging around.

Norman rolls cigarets from canned tobacco, and uses words that come right from college. He has a little touch of exaggeration about his conversation

that adds awe and flavor for the tourist. He can talk oil or Navajo rugs or desert or river with you.

Norman has been playing with the rapids of the San Juan River for years. But it was the expedition of last summer that made him a river man to be reckoned with.

This expedition, in fact, is likely to provide him a livelihood for many years. Because it has publicized his name as a river guide—and it's from the river that Norman mainly makes his living. His summer is scheduled full, and far into the fall.

What Norman does is take summer parties on an eight-day boat ride from Mexican Hat, on the San Juan, clear down to Lee's Ferry, on the Colorado.

He charges $62.50 per person for the eight-day trip, and that includes grub, a cook, sleeping bags, a long taste of the simple outdoor life, much scenery, and many thrills.

On the ninth day, Norman pulls his boats from the water, loads them on trailers, and in one hard day's driving over rough Navajo roads, is back at Mexican Hat.

And on the tenth day, he's headed down river again with a new party. He's practically a street car motorman of the San Juan River. "See the desert by water," is his motto.

He wants to make some kind of hazardous trip late this fall that will hit the front pages again. He hasn't figured out yet just what it will be.

Norman tells some whoppers about the force of the vicious rapids, and I believe them all. For instance, he used to wear a stocking cap on the river. It kept his hair from flying, since the wind doesn't blow it like it would an ordinary hat.

But once, in a particularly bad rapids, the water came deluging the whole boat with such terrific force that it took the stocking cap and pulled it right down over Norman's face, clear down to his neck, and he couldn't see a thing.

Altho rapids-riding is rough going, Nevills says he has never known anybody to be seasick, or perhaps you should say river-sick. Some people, however, have claustrophobia and can't go thru the high-walled canyons.

He says you've either got the knack of handling a boat in rapids, or you haven't. If you've got it, he says he can make a rapids-shooter out of you in three hours.

Nevills says, in all his years on the river, he has never overturned a boat. He says some rivermen contend you have to have spills to learn, but he doesn't agree.

The thing I like most about Nevills is his attitude toward the river. In all these years the river has never nicked him, yet he has an intensely respectful fear of it.

His feeling shows thru everything he does. The great aviators I know are those who are always a little afraid. They're the ones I like to fly with. And so it is with Nevills, and the river he loves and fears.

– July 29, 1939

A LONELY GRAVE IN MONUMENT VALLEY

MONUMENT VALLEY, Utah-Ariz.—We went today down thru Monument Valley, and on into the Valley of Tsay-Bege.

Harry Goulding took us in his car with the big air wheels—the car he can drive right up over the top of sand dunes and not get stuck.

Monument Valley lies smack across the Utah-Arizona line, part in one state, part in the other. It is a vast depression, some 60 miles long and 30 miles wide. It is all Navajo Indian reservation.. The main road, north and south, cuts across the valley.

It is called Monument Valley because in it stand hundreds of monumental stone formations. They grow in this valley like a weird crop. Nowhere else in America will you find them. They are not meticulous and small works of art—they are unbelievably gigantic.

What has happened, really, is that the centuries have eroded out this whole valley; but, standing here and there, fiercely stolid and immovable, are the great masses of rock which resisted nature and would not be eroded.

They have fantastic forms and shapes. Name almost anything you want, and you'll find it's likeness in Monument Valley.

You can see a great medieval castle, or the U.S. Treasury, or a mule lying on its back with its feet up, or the profile of Joseph Smith, the Mormon, or a figure of The Pioneer Woman, or a totem pole, or a pair of mittens.

Distances and shapes are deceptive out here amidst all this space. You can hardly credit the statement that the Castle stands 1400 feet high above the surrounding flats, and that on its level top you could build a whole city.

Most extraordinary of all, to me, is the Totem Pole. It is a solid shaft of rock, sticking straight up out of the desert for more than 700 feet. It stands there all alone, fantastic, impossible, built by nature, and 200 feet higher than the great Washington Monument. To me, it is one of the Seven Wonders of America, and offhand I can't think what the other six are.

In Monument Valley are scores of great natural bridges. There are vast caves, where the Navajo shepherds herd their flocks for refuge. There are weird sandspouts rising into the air.

There are crude ruins of Indian homes a thousand years old. There are sounds, and unearthly presences. Harry Goulding can stand and shout a cowboy whoop, and it comes back many-voiced from all sides, again and again, like a surrounding enemy.

If you knew the countries of the world, you would visit many of them in Monument Valley. You would come around the rocky pinnacle of a butte, and there under the cliff would be a wood-and-mud-hut, and darting thru the door a dark-skinned woman in vividly colored dress, and all around would be sheep and goats grazing and bleating.

The roaming, gypsy shepherds of Arabia—except they're Navajo Indians. Almost as close to 10 centuries ago as the dark shepherds of the Persian deserts. The sight of a camel would surprise you less than the fact that you don't see one.

You see and know only a few of these things if you drive the main north-and-south road across the valley. And yet you must not venture off this road in your own car. They might be days finding you.

The only way to go is with Harry Goulding. Even if it were possible to drive in and out by yourself, still the only way to go is with Harry Goulding. For he is an almost spiritual sexton of Monument Valley, and he transfers his love for it into you.

You spend the whole day in the valley. Much of the time you have no idea where you are. Now you are on old Navajo wagon trails. Now you are on two tracks worn only by Goulding's big air wheels. Sometimes you run down the dry bed of a part-year stream.

Harry stops the car in a peaceful little valley-within-a-valley. We walk a hundred yards. We stop before a pile of brush.

"This man was a friend of mine," Harry Goulding says. "He was a leader among the Indians. See what they sent with him."

There are the bones of a horse. "They knocked the horse in the head," Goulding says, "so its spirit could escape and go with the old man."

And there is a coffee pot, with a hole in the bottom. "They knocked the coffee pot in the head," Goulding says. "And the saddle, too. Everything was knocked in the head, so its spirit could go with the old man."

"I don't know of anything better than being buried out here," said Harry Goulding. "I wouldn't mind if they 'd put me right alongside the old man. I got a few nice things to take along. We could join up when we got there. We'd have a horse and saddle and coffee pot, and we'd knock my car in the head and take it along."

Harry Goulding is right. I've seen great mausoleums, and rows of white crosses by the thousand, and expensive marble shafts and cathedral crypts—but I've never seen the grave of man more peacefully and gently done than that of the old Indian lying in his sandy little valley, rimmed by great rocks, dotted with sage, supplicant to the sun, his simple needs gathered about him. It was beautiful.

– August 3, 1939

THE WETHERILLS OF MONUMENT VALLEY

KAYENTA, Ariz.—Back at Mexican Hat it is the Nevills, and in Monument Valley it's the Gouldings, and here at Kayenta it is the Wetherills.

Even on some of the road maps, under the word, Kayenta you will see printed, in parenthesis, (The Wetherills). And well-deserved that recognition is, too, for they have been here nearly 35 years, even before there was a settlement.

If you come to Kayenta you will stay with the Wetherills. I know you will, for there's no place else to stay. And they can't put up very many, so you'd better stop early.

Their home is a Mexicanish affair——a long one-story strip of rooms, with wings and a hallway running the full length. Inside, it has the atmosphere of antiquity of an old Spanish mission.

John Wetherill is one of four brothers. I am not sure, but I suspect they have had more to do with the discovery of archeological ruins in the Southwest than any scientist.

Since early in the '80s they have been at it. One of the brothers lost his life—the accidental victim of an Indian fracas—and we saw his grave a few days ago out there on the flat bottom of Chaco Canyon in New Mexico.

John Wetherill is best known of the brothers. Books have been written about him. He is getting along now, and takes a nap in the afternoon. He is a smallish man, with a rounded head and a gray mustache. He smokes cigarets, wears a white shirt and tie, and overalls. After supper each evening he has to jump up and go milk a cow.

It was the Wetherills who did most of the early discovery at Mesa Verde Park. They were at Chaco Canyon and Canyon de Chelly, and John Wetherill was in the party that discovered the famous Rainbow Bridge in Utah.

And all these 40 years, hunting Indian ruins has been just a sideline—a hobby—with John Wetherill. His real business, his livelihood, was taking parties of scientists and adventurers on pack trips thruout the Southwest.

It was John Wetherill who, in 1913, led Teddy Roosevelt on the long pack into Rainbow Bridge, for John Wetherill was the only person who knew how to get there.

At the Wetherill's home you eat at a great long table with the family. Their granddaugher will be one of your waitresses. And, after supper, they'll clear off the table and the Indian girl who cooks will come out and play Chinese checkers with the others.

At the head of the table is Mrs. Wetherill, as regal and dominant as a monarch. She commands the situation, speaks with finality to her guests.

Her cigaret poised high, she surveys the assemblage, and joins the repartee with an uncanny mirthless laughter in which her face never changes expression. She is a woman to cope with; a woman to have with you in the frontier life.

There is nothing much at Kayenta except the Wetherills, an Indian school and a fine little Indian hospital for tubercular Navajos.

The only trading post is run in partnership by John Wetherill and Clyde Colville. In the back of their store is the post office. And it is, incidentally, more distant from a railroad than any other post office in the United States.

It is about 145 miles from Kayenta to Flagstaff, the nearest railroad town. And in three other directions—southeast to Gallup, N.M., east to Farmington, N.M., and northeast to Dolores, Colo., the distance doesn't vary by more than 10 miles.

Mail comes twice a week, by truck, from Flagstaff. People from all over America send mail to Kayenta to be posted, because of its small fame on the postal map.

Just before dark a ricketly old car drew up to the Wetherills. A man in overalls got out and asked for water for his canteen. He was a workman on dam

construction jobs, and was moving, with his family, from Colorado to western New Mexico.

They had, that day, driven in their old car across one of the worst roads in the Southwest. The Wetherills gave the man water, and he chugged on into the twilight, to drive these desert paths thruout the night.

When he had gone we spoke of the bad road he had been over—the Mc-Elmo road.

"Have you ever been over that road" I asked Mrs. Wetherill.

Her mouth opened slightly, her expression did not change, only from somewhere came that devastating chuckle. "Have I? By wagon, horseback, afoot, by truck."

You could live in the desert 40 years, and still be a tenderfoot beside Mrs. John Wetherill.

– August 4, 1939

ERNIE GAWKS AND WONDERS

KAYENTA, Ariz.—One of the most astonishing sights in this astonishing country down here is what they term the "Goose Necks of the San Juan."

That isn't a very good term, for the thing resembles a goose's neck about as much as mine does. Which probably isn't a subject we should get into.

This thing is sort of a drunken edition of the Grand Canyon. If I had some paper, I could show you better by drawing a picture, if I only had a pencil.

At any rate, in this one place near Mexican Hat the San Juan River travels six whole miles just to advance one mile. It loops back and forth, as evenly as tho the loops had been made by a machine.

You can stand on the lookout point and look down and, right there in front of you, you can see the river flowing towards you twice, and away from you twice. The canyon at this point is a quarter of a mile deep.

They tell a story about an old Mormon who came down and looked at it. Altho the Mormons are intensely religious, a favorite old-time expression is "My hell!"

So this old Mormon rode up to the lookout point, and stood there gazing awhile, and then he said, "My hell! Where did all them rivers come from?"

Another weird phenomenon at Mexican Hat is none other than Mexican Hat, if you can figure that out. Maybe I'd better help you.

The settlement of Mexican Hat got its name from a queer rock formation just a couple of miles away. It is a huge flat rock, unbelievably balanced on a pedestal, on top of a great cone-shaped butte. Silhouetted against the sky, it looks exactly like a Mexican's big hat upside down. How it balances there without falling off is more than I can tell you.

You can see it plainly from the road, and for miles around. You'd guess that it might be 10 feet across the brim. Actually it is 70 feet, and you could build a house up there. In case you'd like to build, just dial "O" on your telephone and I'll send a man right out.

All thru this country, the white men roll their cigarets. But not out of flake tobacco in sacks, as cowboys do. Out of pipe tobacco, in cans. I couldn't find out why.

In Monticello I bought a plain blue work shirt for 89 cents. It was a little too big, so one night we decided to shrink it.

My friend had to wash out his shirt, so he volunteered to do mine, too. He dipped them good, wrung them out, and then hung them on a chair out on the porch.

He was up long ahead of me next morning. When I got up I walked around the bed, and almost jumped out of my skin at what I saw. For standing there on the floor, standing right straight up all by itself, was my shirt. It was as hard as a board, and full of a million wrinkles, like a mummy. It really looked like some animate thing that had died.

We don't know yet what made the shirt turn so stiff. My friend thought it was the funniest thing he'd ever seen. He had written a note, and pinned it to the shirt. The note said:

"This shirt is the product of the Shaffer New Shirt Softening Process. Let Us Shorten Your New Shirts–The SNSSP."

I think I'll have to throw it away. The shirt, not the note.

Just after you leave Bluff, Utah, there is a big white and black sign of the Utah State Road Commission, with this heartening message on it:

"Fifty-one miles of narrow, steep grades and unbridged washes. Dangerous when in Flood, Be Carefull."

It scares you so badly you can even excuse their poor spelling.

There is no telephone line into Mexican Hat or Monument Valley. There is one, however, here at Kayenta. Except, when we came thru it had been out of kilter for three days. Things are so beautiful down here that they don't even notify headquarters till the third day.

Telegrams come to Kayenta by telephone from Flagstaff. Trader Clyde Colville was telling of an incident that happened to him.

He was called from supper one evening by an urgent message from Flagstaff. It was a telegram, sent from Monticello, Utah. It said to expect two friends there that night to stay all night.

For a minute Mr. Colville couldn't figure it out. Those two friends had been there with him night before last. Then it dawned on him. The telegram had merely been three days traveling the 125 miles from Monticello. The friends had beat it there by two full days! And, you see, it didn't make any difference.

– August 5, 1939

LONG ON LOOKING, SHORT ON TALK

RED LAKE, Ariz.—The night before we left Albuquerque on this long trip into the Navajo country, a newspaper friend brought us what purported to be a news story hot off the teletype machine.

It told how a party of 13 tourists had been set upon by the Indians, six of them being killed and the other seven escaping minus their scalps.

It wasn't, of course, a news story at all. Our friend had written it out himself, and we all had a big laugh over it.

So we went to the other extreme, scoffed at Indian savagery, and dubbed ourselves "The Navajo Extinction Expedition of 1939." Said we, "If there's any scalping, we'll do it."

"Yeah," said our cynical friend. "I know what'll happen. You'll get up there in the wilds and those Navajos will sell you a lot of third-rate rugs at double tourist prices."

Of course, none of these things has come to pass. We haven't scalped anybody, haven't been scalped, and haven't even bought any rugs. We've seen hundreds of Indians and you consider it the climax of a perfect day if you can even get one to speak to you.

I don't know anything about Indians, and doubt that I ever will. Some white people down here go sort of Indian-daffy. They make a fad of the Indians; consider them utterly superior to the white man. Others dislike the Indians thoroly. The more understanding whites respect them for their qualities of simple goodness.

As for myself, I have tried, and tried hard, to get interested in Indians. It is no go. I am not what you would call anti-Indian. I'm merely non-Indian. I can't help it. It's just the way my nature runs.

So when I write about Indians it will be based only on what white people have told me.

The Navajos are the biggest tribe of Indians in America. They number now around 50,000 and are increasing all the time. They are a pastoral people, constantly moving with their sheep and cattle and horses.

The Navajos still stick close to the beliefs and customs of old. They do not have towns nor permanent homes. They move several times a year, herding their flocks here and there. They build a new house, or '"hogan," wherever they go. The "hogan" is a round, one-roomed hut, made of logs and brush and chinked with mud.

When a Navajo dies in his house, it is never used again. The family smashes in the back of the house, and there it stands till it falls down. It is sacred and taboo.

Sometimes white men will come and tear down the ruins, and use the logs for firewood. The Indians don't object. But they wouldn't go into a house heated by that wood.

You could go out into the desert, take some logs from a deserted hogan, and build yourself a campfire and boil some coffee. The Indians would sit at a distance and watch you, and there would be no hard feelings over your tearing down the spirit-ridden hogan.

But they would not think of getting close enough to absorb any of the heat from that fire, and they would not drink a cup of coffee boiled over it, even if they were starving.

Indians have lots of horses. People tell me a Navajo measures his wealth by the number of horses he has. Yet the Indian doesn't have any use for more than a couple of horses. The result is that the ranges are full of Navajo ponies, eating their heads off and doing nobody the slightest good.

The Government has recently started a horse-reduction program, to free the sparse ranges for the Navajos' sheep. Those who know say it is a wholly worthy program.

But the Indians don't like it. The newspapers are carrying pieces about how wonderfully the Indians are co-operating. Range riders and traders tell me that is not the truth.

Just before the program started, a horse buyer came thru a certain section. He was offering $10 and $12 a head for horses. He didn't get many. The Indians wouldn't sell.

But in a few weeks they'll have to sell those same horses for $2 a head, to be made into fertilizer and dog food. That's your Indian co-operation—and foresight.

If you come thru this country as a tourist, the thing that will impress you most is the way the Indians stare at you.

It isn't a stare of curiosity. They see plenty of white people. It's an unearthly steady stare, like somebody in a trance. They just stare you to death.

We met an Indian riding a horse. He was the stariest one yet. We waved, but he just kept staring. His horse jumped and plunged, but he never took his eyes off us.

I believe if he had fallen off his horse and rolled over, he would have kept that stare directed right at us, like a contortionist holding a glass of water on his head.

— August 7, 1939

NAVAJOS NEED A PRESS AGENT

TUBA CITY, Ariz.—Of course the Indian Bureau has done some mighty fine work, in its way, but it took a genius like me to come thru here and solve this Navajo problem at a glance.

What the Navajo Indians need more than anything else is Steve Hannagan.

Here's the idea:

The Navajos occupy a reservation that is roughly 100 miles square. Most of it is in Arizona, but it extends north into Utah and east into New Mexico.

It is a sparse, dry land, and the one great question as you travel thru is, "How in the world does anybody make a living here?"

Yet the desert is deceptive, and life can be abundant on what appears to the untrained eye an utter waste. The Navajos run great flocks of sheep. We were constantly startled by the fatness of the flocks and the butter-ball condition of their horses.

But still, the Navajos are poor. They don't even have enough to eat, we are told. They are intensely susceptible to tuberculosis. Undernourishment drags them down. They need a more abundant market for the things they have to sell.

Now, Navajo ponies are the prettiest little pieces of horseflesh you ever saw. They're excellent horses, too; good-natured, wiry, and tough as steel. Big enough for anybody; yet small enough to fall easily into a certain niche as "faddish."

The Navajos are overrun with horses. But the rest of America doesn't know anything about them.

A good, high-powered press agent, going at it the right way, could make the East Navajo-pony-conscious. He could make Navajo ponies fashionable, like Doberman dogs.

He could have the rest of this country buying thousands of Navajo ponies every year if the Indians would condescend to sell. And he could run the price up to a fancy $50 per head instead of the present $2 for dogfood.

So much for the horses. That isn't all the press agent could do. Take Navajo rugs.

I'm sort of a bug on Navajo rugs. When we're in the Southwest I just have to shut my eyes and grit my teeth to keep from buying Navajo rugs. If I were rich I'd buy scores of them and give them to friends.

The Southwest is fully conscious of the beauty of these rugs. You seldom go into a white home in these parts without finding it saturated with Navajo rugs.

But outside of this, and those picked up by a few suddenly enthusiastic tourists, the market for Navajo rugs is not great.

As one trader said, anybody in the United States who can afford a nice home could do well with an Indian room in it. Not because he's Indian-crazy, but simply because a room of Navajo rugs and Indian trinkets is a pleasant room, a room of softness and grace.

The Indians could make a lot more rugs than they do. A good metropolitan press agent could sell America on Navajo rugs. It might not only help the Indians, it might sweep up into a great buying boom that would pull is back to prosperity, stop wars, keep submarines from sinking, bring rain and make me an honorary member of the Navajo tribe.

Think it over, Indians.

All Navajo rugs are made by women. And they're made from the wool of the sheep the Navajos raise. The designs all mean something in Indian tradition. And the nice part is that it's absolutely against the gods for a woman ever to make two rugs alike.

The most prominent of the Navajo symbols is the swastika. They tell a story out here of a new clerk in one of the Indian trading posts who sent back in high dudgeon a bunch of blankets that had swastikas on them. He was either fired, or should have been. The swastika was a Navajo emblem centuries before Hitler ever thought of it.

The tourists never buy rugs from the Indians themselves. They do all their selling to the trading posts. All the rugs you see in the fancy shops in Albuquerque and Gallup and Flagstaff have first come thru the hands of traders.

And, like oranges in California, you find the poorest selection of rugs right out here where they're actually made. The best ones are shipped off for sale in the cities.

When a rug is finished, the Indian man gets on his horse, rides to a trading post, bargains with the trader, arrives at a price and takes that much out in supplies.

That's the reason all the stores in this country go by the name of "trading posts." The merchants trade supplies to the Indians for their rugs.

It takes a lot of time to trade with an Indian. He'll sit and think all day. He'll ride in for 30 miles to trade off a $3 rug. He'll hang around two or three days and nights while the dickering goes on. He'll up and ride another 50 miles to get an extra dime.

That's all I can think of about Navajo ponies and rugs. I won't be surprised if some day you find me sitting out in Monument Valley behind a sage bush, weaving a Navajo rug myself.

— August 8, 1939

BLUFF CALLS THE ROAD "SLOW"

CAMERON, Ariz.—When we started this long-drawn-out trip into the desert country of New Mexico, Utah and Arizona, we prepared ourselves as tho we were going from the Cape to Cairo.

We replaced two worn tires with new ones. We bought a shovel. We carried a five-gallon can of water for the radiator and a gallon thermos jug for ourselves.

We bought a tire pump, a can of patches, an extra fan belt and two quarts of oil. We took a first aid kit, and a snake bite kit. We had a funnel and a tin cup.

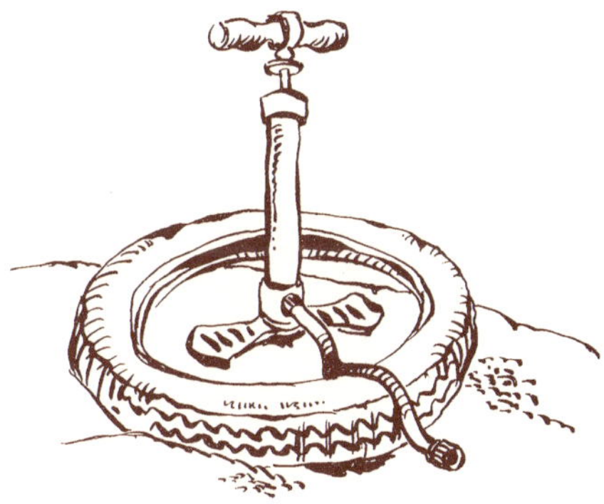

We had a small board on which to place the jack in the sand. We had a roll of old gunny sacks to put under the wheels if we got stuck. We had two cans of sardines and a box of crackers, just in case.

We had a .22 rifle and a German Luger revolver. These were just for fun, and not because we thought we'd need them. We wore overalls and heavy shoes.

This sounds like a lot, yet we got it all in the baggage compartment, and didn't have a thing strapped on or hanging outside the car.

Now the desert trip is over. Of all this paraphernalia, we had no need for anything except the two cans of water, the funnel and the tin cup.

We never even saw a snake. We never saw anything to shoot at except some prairie dogs. We didn't eat our sardines and the fan belt didn't break.

Yet if I were making this trip again, I wouldn't eliminate a single thing. For it is entirely possible to need all these things in the desert, and when you need them you need them bad.

Most important of all, I would say, are water, good tires, a shovel and a tire pump.

We never did get stuck in the sand, but we came close to it a number of times. Twice we had to stop and let the radiator boil, and each time it took about a gallon of water.

Our thermos jug was indispensable. Nearly every day we carried our lunch, fixed for us at wherever we stayed the night before.

These dirt roads thru the Navajo reservation are not what you would go on for a Sunday afternoon's spin. Yet they are not as bad as we expected.

The worst part was the 10 miles between Bluff and Comb Wash, in Utah. As they term it in Bluff, the road is "slow." My term for it would be—"It stinks."

You're in second or low gear much of the time. You're driving across acres of solid sheet rock. You're thru sand to the hubs. You're all the time so up-and-downish you can hardly sit in the car. Sometimes the steering wheel is jerked out of your hand.

And when you finally make the summit of Comb Ridge, and swing around a hairpin turn, you are suddenly and surprisingly confronted with the steepest down-grade I've ever been on.

They call it Navajo Hill. It is just wide enough for one car. The thing gave me a terrific start. I threw into second gear, and then into low, and used both brakes.

I don't see how some of these old cars ever get up it, going the other way.

They differ locally on just how steep it is. After we were down in the valley we stopped and looked back, and tried to judge. We figured at least 25 degrees. But the boys around Mexican Hat say it is 32 degrees.

We laughed many times at what appears to be a road rivalry between Utah and Arizona. Every single person we met in Utah would say exactly this:

"The roads are all right till you hit Arizona, and then they're pretty bad."

And the truth is that nowhere on the Arizona side did we find roads as bad as in Utah.

The main worry, all along, is about getting stuck in the sand. If you do, above everything don't sit there and spin your wheels. You'll just get stuck deeper and deeper.

Get out, shovel a channel ahead of your wheels, gather some sage brush and make a carpet of it in the channel, let the air out of your tires down to about 15 pounds, be sure that your front wheels are headed straight, and then get in and drive out.

Most new cars today aren't equipped with tire pumps. But you should carry a pump in the desert, to pump up your tires if you have to let the air out of them.

The best months for a trip thru this country are June and September and October. The rains come in July and August. You can get thru during the rainy season if you know your stuff. But if you're a novice in this country, as I am, it's better to stay out during July and August.

We didn't suffer at all from the heat. But, of course, we're sort of hot weather maniacs. In fact, a couple of nights I had to go out and chase Indians to keep my blood circulating.

— August 9, 1939

ERNIE DOESN'T KNOW WHAT TO SAY

GRAND CANYON, Ariz. (South Rim) —By diligent spying and listening, I have found out what most people say when they see the Grand Canyon for the first time.

As for me, I didn't say anything. In fact, I wasn't seeing it for the first time. My first view of the Grand Canyon was from an airplane 10 years ago.

But, of course, I was just a little tyke then, not even 30 years old, and I don't remember much about it. So today, you might say, was really my first modern view of Grand Canyon, and absolutely my first one from the ground.

As we stood there on the rim, gazing at this gigantic spectacle created by nature, I knew I should utter some profound observation for prosperity. But I couldn't think of a thing.

Other people have less trouble with their tongues, however. Nearly everybody makes some sort of remark. As far as I can gather, they run about in this order:

1. "What a shock the first men who saw it must have had." (The Imaginists.)

2. "I'm afraid the Soil Erosion Service got here too late." (The Wits.)

3. "How insignificant it makes man feel." (The Philosophers.)

Wondering about the emotions of the first man seems to go thru everybody's mind. It did mine too. It must have given him an awful start.

If you were walking thru this country on foot, you would approach the canyon thru heavy forests. You wouldn't have the slightest warning there was anything unusual ahead.

And then you'd push aside a bush, and there just as suddenly as a gunshot, you'd be looking down into the most colossal hole on this old earth. I don't see how the first man kept from falling in, just from sheer nightmarish surprise.

The first white visitor, however, was here so long ago there isn't any record of what he thought or said. And even if he said something, it was in Spanish. And unless he said "Buenos noches, Señor," which hardly seems likely, I wouldn't have understood it.

Don Lopez de Cardenas and 12 other Spaniards in the Coronado Expedition, up from Mexico, get the credit for discovering the Canyon. That was 1540.

It was nearly 300 years later that the first Americans saw the Canyon. James O. Pattie, a beaver trapper, and his father, explored clear along the south rim in 1826.

Of all the ruins and geologic phenomena that I have seen, Grand Canyon is by far the oldest. It's so old that scientists have no idea how old. And it is so big they can't even measure its present rate of erosion, if any.

But it has been here so terribly long that it is quite likely that it looked to the Spaniards 400 years ago exactly as it does today. And if you could see it a thousand years from now, you probably couldn't pick out any change with the naked eye.

The American Automobile Association guidebook says of Grand Canyon that in its power to rouse the emotions it has no equal in the world.

With that statement I am inclined to disagree. The Canyon kind of overdoes itself. Time after time I've heard visitors say, "Well, it's just too big to appreciate." And frequently I've heard them say they were more impressed with Carlsbad Caverns or Bryce Canyon Park.

It is my own feeling that the thing is too gigantic for human emotions to get hold of. You look at it, and there she is, awful beautiful and awful big, and you're just about stopped right there.

The Canyon averages about 10 miles across. There are places where it is 18 miles wide.

And in its very bottom, where the Colorado River runs, it is a mile deep.

There are so many hundreds of canyons within the main canyon, and so many ridges and buttes and what-not still standing in that vast depression that it is only from certain points on the rim that you can even catch a glimpse of the river way off down there.

Standing on the South Rim, you can pick out a little trail way down in the canyon. If you look hard, you can see a few dark specks barely moving on the trail.

Then if you look thru the telescope mounted on the wall, those specks turn out to be trail-workmen on mules. Even thru the telescope you can just make them out—that's how far down it is.

There is a great hotel-lodge standing on the North Rim, 14 miles across. You cannot find it with the naked eye. You can finally spot it thru the telescope, if you are patient .

If your visit here has to be a short one, looking thru that telescope is about the most fun of all. I don't see why the Government doesn't put up half a dozen of them.

— August 15, 1939

PYLE DECIDES TO POSTPONE CROSSING

GRAND CANYON, Ariz. (North Rim) —Here is an example of what a whopper the Grand Canyon really is.

When you stand at the Lodge here on the North Rim, you are only 14 miles from the hotel on the South Rim. Yet if you want to drive over there, you have to drive 215 miles around the east end of the canyon, or 618 miles around the west end, over Boulder Dam. And if you send a letter from one rim to the other, it takes four days to get there.

You can, however, cross the canyon in two days, if you want to take yourself a real trip. You go by muleback. It costs you $30, and for that you get a mule, a guide, your meals, and overnight lodging at Phantom Ranch in the bottom of the canyon.

I had thought of taking this trip myself, just for the experience. But two things stopped me— the $30 and fright.

"Is the trail scary?" I asked the man at the hotel desk.

"No it isn't scary," he said. "Of course, there are stretches where you look straight down for a thousand feet. But the trail is eight feet wide, and you couldn't push a mule off with a locomotive."

My great worry is not over the mule staying on the trail. My worry is about me staying on the mule. I decided to wait till I got braver.

The North Rim of the canyon is a different world from the South Rim. It is 1000 feet higher, so high in fact that it's chilly all summer long. There are no nights when you don't sleep under blankets, and shiver in the evening. The North Rim is about 8500 feet above sea level.

I like the North Rim best. It isn't so crowded. You feel more of nature over here. The great central lodge run by the Union Pacific is magnificent. But you don't have that Coney Island feeling you get on the South Rim.

True, the view of the Canyon from the North Rim is not as good as from the South. But to me the North Rim is a place where you wouldn't mind spending a vacation; while on the South Rim my feeling is to look, and move on.

One odd thing about the Grand Canyon is that most people think its in Colorado. Used to think so myself. Don't know where we get that idea— I suppose it's because the canyon is made by the Colorado River.

But the Grand Canyon itself is wholly, thoroly and complete in Arizona. And don't let anybody tell you it isn't.

Having myself already passed thru that feverish malady known as amateur photography, I can now sit back in silent placidity and enjoy the antics of those who are still in the horrible throes of taking pictures of everything.

We ran onto a very bad case here today. We went out with a tourist party, where you sit on logs on the rim of the canyon and listen to a geological lecture by the Ranger.

In the party was one man who did no listening. He was too busy. He didn't even give his wife time to listen. He had one of those tourist's eyeshades, turned backward on his head. He had five cameras.

Yes, I said five cameras. Everything from a pocket Leica to a big movie machine on a tripod. And he used them all. He was a regular Benny Goodman of amateur photography.

Most people don't know it, but there is a tribe of Indians living right in the bottom of Grand Canyon. They are Havasupais. There are about 200 of them.

As I understand it, they were chased down there by bad Indians back in the '80s and have never come out. A white Indian agent stays down there with them.

I asked an old cowboy about them—whether they were smart or not. He was the kind of cowboy who would never say anything bad about anybody. Of the Havasupais' intelligence he said, "Well, I'd say it's about average. Yes, just about average." Meaning I judge that there aren't any Einsteins down there.

The only way to get down to these Indians is by mule or foot over an 11-mile trail. Some day, you bet your life, I'm going down there to see them. Maybe I'll stay down there, too, you can't tell.

— August 16, 1939

RETRIBUTION OVERTAKES ERNIE

ZION NATIONAL PARK, Utah—There is something terribly ironic about Zion Park. I don't know whether I ought to tell it or not.

Oh, come now, Ernest, tell us what it is. Well, I don't know if I should. Aw, you're scared to tell. No I ain't. Then why don't you tell us? Well, I ain't exactly scared but Mr. Ickes won't like it. Aw, we won't tell nobody. Well, if I gotta. It's this—

The Government spent a million dollars to build a road so people could get into see the Park, and the way it turned out the road is more wonderful than the Park.

There I've gone and done it. I'll bet I catch it now. I didn't want to say it in the first place, and you made me.

But it's the truth. The road is so marvelous that the park is an anti-climax.

It took them, if I remember, three years to build the road. It goes thru a tunnel more than a mile long. Of course there are lots of tunnels in the world, but this tunnel . . .

It slopes all the way, and it has curves in it, and that isn't all. Every once in a while they've blasted out a big cave in the side of the tunnel, that leads out to outdoors, and you can pull your car over and look right out into the great canyon where you're going.

The A.A.A. Bluebook lists this road as one of the finest engineering achievements in American highway building. Everybody talks about it. Everybody admires it. It is superb.

The road cuts off scores of miles of driving, and allows you to enter the the Park from the east side as well as from the west. It also enables you to see Bryce Canyon and Zion Park and Grand Canyon all in a day, instead of hanging around awhile and appreciating them as you should.

There is one thing about Zion Park—it has relieved me of a queer obsession.

You know there are some scientists who spend all their time worrying about the world running out of oil. And others fret about the eventual exhaustion of all our coal. And still others spend a lifetime stewing over the day when our forests will all be gone.

Well, I'm like that. Only I have a field all to myself. I have always worried about running out of rock. I've even caught myself sitting up in bed at night, screaming "My God, we're out of rock!"

But now my worries are over. For today we've seen enough rock to keep all the armies and contractors and little boys of the world in rock till the end of time.

There are whole mountains of solid rock here. And I don't mean big rough-looking rock covered with trees and gullies and dirt, like the Canadian Rockies.

I mean just bare, slick, clean, hard rock—as far as you can see, nothing at all but rock. The slopes and valleys and even the creek beds are solid rock. You drive for miles and you won't even see two bucketfuls of dirt.

All this fantastic rock business is on the east side of the tunnel I told you about, before you get into Zion Canyon. Once you get there, there isn't much left to see.

There's a very pretty canyon, and the beautiful stone dwellings of the park people, and the pretty lodge of the Union Pacific. And Weeping Rock.

The Rangers said I must leave the car and walk up and see Weeping Rock. A dirt trail winds up thru weeds and bushes. It's only about two blocks off the road.

Well, I got within a few yards of the Rock, I guess. And all of a sudden a snake stuck his head out of the weeds at me.

I yelled and jumped and then composed myself and got three rocks, each about the size of my fist.

The first one I just tossed into the weeds where I thought the snake was; a sort of exploratory rock. It brought results. A head stuck up above the weeds.

So I took a nice nervous aim, and whammed the second rock. It missed the head about two feet and anyway it turned out to be a lizard. But—

That rock did arouse the real snake. And there all of a sudden I saw him coming thru the weeds right at me. I suppose snake-lovers would say he was just curious, but I say he was full of criminal intent. His head was way up.

I had one brief moment of catalepsy. Then I opened my mouth about a foot, gave out one of those banshee howls I sometimes use in nightmares, let the rock fly, and leaped 30 feet back down the trail, all in one movement.

On the witness stand, I suppose I could not prove that the rock hit the snake, because I wasn't there by that time. But the last I saw of the rock, it was going mighty straight.

Something tells me there's one less snake in the world than there was this morning. And something also tells me there is one guy who will never get to see Zion Park's famous Weeping Rock.

So that is the saga of my day in Zion. I'm afraid it doesn't sound very good.

And I'm sorry too. Because Paul Frank, the park superintendent, was awfully nice to me, and we had a good lunch at the cafeteria, and I love the Union Pacific Railroad, and I found out all about all that rock. But can I help it if snakes chase me?

– August 17, 1939

DAME NATURE GOES MAD

BRYCE CANYON PARK, Utah—Bryce Canyon had better get busy and sue Walt Disney for plagiarism, or vice versa. Either Walt is copying Nature, or Nature is copying Walt. Bryce Canyon is a Silly Symphony, standing still.

Fantastic is the word for Bryce Canyon. It just doesn't seem real. It's as tho Nature decided to stop being so serious, and took half a day off and made crazy stuff and daubed it up with pretty colors and had a wonderful time.

Bryce Canyon is a sort of Carlsbad Cavern outdoors. You stand on the rim of a precipice. You look down into a valley. And in this valley is a regular forest of tall and erratically carved stone spires, rising as high as 500 feet.

En masse, they look like a huge forest of gigantic stone tree trunks, without limbs. Or they look like a solar pipe-organ. Or they look like ten thousand pink flagpoles. Or they look like what you see if somebody hits you on the head with a mallet.

All these poles have weird knots and projections and top-pieces on them. It is probably the best spot in the world for just sitting and picking out images. You can find a camel, or Williams Jennings Bryan. It is better than seeing faces in clouds or in fireplaces.

The Rangers tell me you'd be surprised at the number of tourists who ask, in complete seriousness, if the CCC boys have carved all these figures from the rock.

It is erosion, of course. But how Nature could take a few acres of land and wash it away till the floor lay 500 feet below, and yet leave thousands of slim stone poles sticking up there unharmed, is beyond me.

The over-all color is pink. But there are white spots, and dark spots, and colors change as the day wears on. The finest time for looking is just before sundown. Then the dark shadows of these thousands of spires reach across each other, and they make a scene of such chaotic fantasy that you just have to stand there and look till the light is gone. You wouldn't be surprised to hear flutes.

I don't know why they call it a canyon, for it isn't really a canyon. It's just a high mesa, and then a sudden drop off into a valley, and then the valley opens out and falls away an the far side to a vast rich plain. It's a one-sided canyon, that's what it is.

The park itself is long and narrow, following this rim for some 25 miles. These spectacular formations are close to the wall. They grow in patches—a patch here and another patch a few miles along. They are like the scattered garden patches of a mountain farmer.

The biggest and most spectacular is just over the rim from Bryce Canyon Lodge. You can either stand at the lookout building and just gawk in comfort, or you can take the trail and walk down among them.

The most-used trail is a circular trip to the bottom and back, covering a mile and a half. You are always urged, of course, to get down there and look up. But I must report disappointedly that it's crazier and prettier from on top.

It took Ranger Fred Brueck and me three-quarters of an hour to walk this mile and a half trail and back out again. We didn't hurry, of course.

But the other day a fellow showed up and said he had just made it in 15 minutes.

The Rangers didn't say so, but they were immensely skeptical. That's averaging six miles an hour, and two-thirds of the distance is a very steep uphill pull.

So the next morning Ranger Brueck and one of his friends decided to try it out. They are both young fellows of college age; athletic, long-winded. They walk hundreds of miles a year, and run ski-trails in the winter. They are in the pink.

So they started out. They ran all the way to the bottom. They came back up as fast as athletic muscles could pull them. They didn't stop to rest.

When they got to the top they were absolutely washed out and done in. And it had taken them 17 minutes. They consider that 15-minute tourist a —— ——— ——— liar!

Bryce Canyon is named after Ebenezer Bryce, a Mormon cattleman who settled down in the valley, at the edge of the spired tanglework, in 1875. The rest of his life was spent here.

Just before Cattleman Bryce died, he was approached to give a description of the canyon. They felt that his close association with it over so many years should bring forth a descriptive phrase that would live with the park for many years. They were right. Ebenezer thought a long time, and then he said.

"Well, it's a hell of a place to lose a cow."

— August 18, 1939

THE DOCTOR WHO NEVER SENDS A BILL

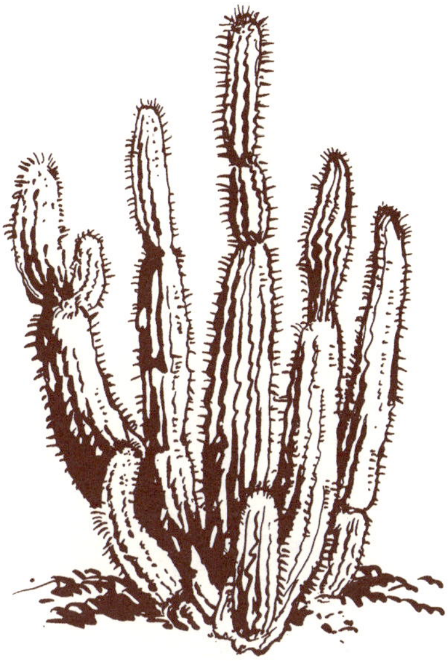

SHERMAN, N.M.—If you were to go about asking people, from the poorest desert rat to the richest banker, who is the most wonderful man in southwestern New Mexico, I am sure you would get but one answer. It would be:

"Why, Doctor Stovall, of course."

Dr. Richard F. Stovall has been the sage and the saviour of Mimbres Valley for more than 30 years. He is an excellent physician, and a man who has literally given his life to helping people, without giving a hoot about the money.

Dr. Stovall was born in Texas, but he went to medical school in Louisville, Ky. After his graduation he served a year at a "lunatic asylum," as he calls it, in Louisville.

And then he came out here. That was in 1884. He set up in Deming, N.M., two years after that town was founded. "No, I didn't come for my health," he says. "My health was fine. I came to make a living."

He was company doctor for the Southern Pacific Railroad. Then he spent 10 years in Mexico as company doctor for a big American mine. He still likes the Mexican people. And they worship him.

Dr. Stovall's life in these sparsely settled spaces has been an epic. He has ridden as far as 150 miles on horseback to tend a sick man. He has fixed up broken jaws with the wire from old-fashioned beer-bottle tops.

There were still raiding Indians in those early days. If Dr. Stovall got a message for a long ride across the mountains, he wouldn't go in the daytime. He'd wait till darkness and then ride all night, to escape the Indians. He never carried a gun.

In those days practically all his surgery was done right on the spot. The kitchen table of a rancher's home was the operating table. He'd boil all the

sheets in the house for swabs. He'd get a cowboy to give an anesthetic, and a Mexican boy to hold a lantern.

He has performed thousands of operations like that. And altho he has naturally lost cases, he never lost one from infection in these crude operations.

Ranchers and Mexicans and miners and squatters by the thousand owe their lives to Dr. Stovall. Yet he has never kept a book and never sent a bill. He has received checks for medical services as much as 30 years after the services were performed. People paid what they could and when they could.

Many years ago Dr. Stovall's practice became so extensive that he built a sanitarium here in the valley along the Mimbres River. Water comes out of the springs at 130 degrees, and has healing powers for diseases of the nerves and muscles.

His office is here, and his home. It is far from any main highway, at the end of a dirt road. Yet in summer the place is full to its capacity of 35 patients.

And thru all these 55 years of doctoring in the isolated Southwest, Dr. Stovall has kept up. He reads everything that happens in the medical world. At least once a year he has taken trips to California or New York, visiting hospitals, taking refresher courses.

They say out here that in the medical conventions the doctors yawn and whisper and wander away as speakers drone on and on. But, they say, when Dr. R. F. Stovall gets up to speak the hall is always packed and the doctors sit on the edge of their chairs.

Dr. Stovall prides himself most on his thoroness as a diagnostician. Anybody can treat a case if he knows what to treat. It's finding out what the trouble actually is, that is fundamental. If you diagnose wrong, it's like taking the wrong road.

Today Dr. Stovall lives with his daughter and her husband not far from the sanitarium. Bill Graham, his son-in-law, runs the ranch. Dr. Stovall owns about 1500 acres of land, and has more than 15 sections under grazing lease. His cattle are all thorobreds.

He loves to hunt. For more than 20 years he and three cronies have gone deer-hunting in the mountains each fall. But he had to miss this year.

For Dr. Stovall has been very ill this summer. He lay unconscious in Silver City Hospital for almost six weeks. Just as he was getting better, Mrs. Stovall died. The whole country was worried sick about Dr. Stovall.

So when we came out to see him I expected to find a man very feeble, very old, very weatherbeaten. I was never more surprised.

For he shows no age at all. He is short, heavily built, and with a full head of curly steel-gray hair. He neither looks nor acts old. He talks slowly and deliberately, and a sharp little caustic wit springs thru his conversation.

But oddest of all he bears no marks whatever of a pioneer country doctor whose life has been spent on horses and in the winds and sun of the Southwest.

His hands are white and unwrinkled and neatly manicured. His face is neither bronzed nor leathery. His clothes are not old man's clothes, but the kind you see in Esquire. He smokes cigars. You could take him for a Fifth Ave. surgeon. Except that Fifth Ave. surgeons keep books and send bills.

— November 7, 1939

SEVEN BURROS, 44 DOGS

PHOENIX, Ariz.—Scotty is an Australian. He went to sea when he was just a boy, and he was at sea for 40 years. Then 18 years ago he left the sea and came to the United States for good. He is getting along in years now.

Scotty lives under a tree out beyond the east edge of Phoenix. He does not live alone by any means. He as one of the biggest families I've ever seen. It consists of—

Seven burros, three goats, and 44 dogs. And Scotty loves them every one.

Scotty never wears any clothes. None, that is, except a scant pair of shorts, made by cutting off the legs of an old pair of overalls.

He is a man of average size, but age has not wrinkled him. His chest is large, and his arms are muscular and unwrinkled. He is as tanned as a Miami debutante. And all over his arms and legs, sweeping blue tattooed figures chase each other.

Scotty's hair is white and long, and his beard, too. Most of the day it is scraggly and full of thistles and weeds. But after his daily plunge in the canal Scotty combs it out, and it lies straight and white and clean.

Scotty and his family live mainly from the garbage dumps. That is abetted occasionally by a handout from a nearby slaughterhouse, and from a gang of good-hearted WPA workmen. And once a month he gets a check for $8—Arizona's old-age pension.

Then Scotty and his family put on the dog. He buys groceries and meat. He cooks up 20 pounds of hamburger and the dogs have a feast. Then he goes back to the garbage dump.

Scotty is, obviously, different from the run of people. But he's pleasant to talk to, and he is smart. His eyes are that uncanny gray-blue of the desert; his vocabulary is excellent; when he shakes hands, he takes your hand in both of his.

He says he lives the way he does because that's the only way he can be free. If he put on clothes and ate well and had some change in his pocket he'd have to pay for it by a thousand little regimentations. As it is, he's as free as a mouse, and just as poor.

Scotty's real name is Alfred Llewellyn Wallace. "But just forget the Llewellyn," he says. There is Scottish in him, and Irish. He hasn't heard from his relatives in Australia for many years. If his mother is still living, she is past 100 now. The last time he saw her she weighed 49 pounds. He never expects to see Australia again.

When Scotty forsook the sea in favor of a covered wagon shortly after the World War, he took a long wagon journey to the East. He went to New York. It took him four years.

For several years now he hasn't left Arizona. In the summer he goes up into the hills around Prescott. In winter he comes back to the warmth of the Phoenix Valley.

Each of Scotty's 44 dogs is named. He knows each one by sight. Not only that, he can shut his eyes and tell you, just by the sound, the name of the one that's barking.

When he's on the road he carries a bucket of lime water. Every evening he cleans and sterilizes the wagon where the dogs ride. Then he dips each dog into a bucket of creosote solution and massages it all over. That keeps them from having mange.

Scotty has had two of his three goats for 18 years. One is an Australian goat. Scotty squats down in front of it and says, "Scratch my back." The goat with apparent delight, rubs its head up and down on Scotty's bare back. "Now scratch it crossways," he says. The goat then rubs the other way.

Scotty sleeps only two hours a night—just after midnight. Two hours is all he needs, he says. The other 22 hours he is hard at work rustling grub for his huge family.

He must be an eerie sight out there in the red glow of the trash heaps at night, nearly naked, his white hair and beard all awry, a big sack on his arm, rummaging and digging in the discard of mankind.

Scotty himself is seldom sick, and he says he doesn't get cold. But there is still Congo malaria in him, and when that hits, he shakes and shivers till the ground rattles.

Around Scotty's neck is a little chain, and on the end of it a crucifix.

"I'm a Roman Catholic," Scotty says, "but not a very good one. I don't go to mass or make confession. But two Fathers and Sister come down to see me once in a while. The Catholics are good about things like that."

Scotty can quote poetry from Shelley or Keats, and if you're interested he'll stand and give you a "reading" of one of his own poems about the open road and the green fields. "If I get despondent, I write poetry, or sing," he says.

Scotty doesn't know whether there is a hereafter or not, but he goes on this assumption:

If there is, he has earned his ticket; and if there isn't, well, at least people will remember him only with kindness when he's gone. What's wrong with that?

– November 25, 1939

HAPPINESS IN DESERT CAVES

DEATH VALLEY, Calif.—On your California road maps you will see a place called Cave Springs.

Yet when you get there you find it is not a town. It is not a village. It is not even a country post office. It is just a private home, with two people in it. It's on the map because it's the only house in a stretch of 140 miles.

Mrs. Ira Sweetman and her cousin, Adrian Egbert, live there. It is 60 miles to a store in one direction, 80 miles in the other. Either way, it's all desert. There are no phone poles, no culverts. Sometimes you can hardly tell where the dirt road is.

"Do many travelers use this road?" I asked Mr. Egbert

"Yes," he said. "There was a car past here just the other day."

Mrs. Sweetman and Mr. Egbert live in this bare,out-of-the-way place completely by choice. They don't have to raise anything, or scratch for a living. They are simply retired.

They are getting along in years (between 65 and 70, I'd say) , but they're alive and enthusiastic, they're well-to-do in a modest way, they have every comfort, and they're on the desert because they like it.

They live in a fascinating place. They're in a gap in the mountains, 3600 feet high. From their door you look down into fabulous Death Valley, below sea level. At night you can see a campfire 55 miles away on the valley floor.

Their home is perched on the south rim of Death Valley. And on the north rim, 130 miles away, is the isolated castle of Death Valley Scotty.

The Sweetman-Egbert menage has none of the fame of Scotty's castle. And yet it is just as isolated, and just as unusual, too. For while Scotty lives in an incongruously lavish palace, they live mostly in caves!

I know it will be hard for you to think of desert cave dwellers as being sane, intelligent, educated people. But try to take my word for it, because it's true. You wouldn't know Mrs. Sweetman or Mr. Egbert from a couple of good Indiana neighbors.

We drew up at Cave Springs just at noon, after the 60-mile pull from Barstow. I knocked at the door, and asked Mrs. Sweetman if she could furnish us a bit of lunch.

"Why yes," she said. "Come right on in. This is Mr. Egbert. I look a sight. Sit down and make yourselves at home. We're just getting ready to have a bite ourselves. We never eat much for lunch."

So they put on another can of chile con carne, and got out a special bunch of celery and pretty soon we were all around the kitchen table, eating sausages and yams and chile and coffee and a dish of figs, just like old times.

We stayed three hours, and they showed us all thru their amazing place, and got out old letters and pictures, and we talked, talked, talked, and would have been there yet, I suppose, except that Mr. Egbert told Mrs. Sweetman she'd have to stop talking and make us go on, or we wouldn't get to Furnace Creek before dark.

Mrs. Sweetman and Mr. Egbert have both been around. Mrs. Sweetman first saw daylight in Richmond, Va. But when she was 10 she migrated with her parents to the Black Hills of South Dakota.

A good part of her life was spent there, and she owns stock in the famous Homestake gold mine at Lead, S.D. She loves the Black Hills. Occasionally she goes to Los Angeles to attend the banquets of the Black Hills Pioneer Society.

"I never knew I was a pioneer till they started making over me a few years ago," she says. "And now I'm kind of proud of it."

Mrs. Sweetman has been a widow for 20 or 30 years. She likes politics, and has been an active political leader in both South Dakota and Arizona. For several years she was postmistress at Daggett, Calif., on the Mojave Desert. She and her cousin came to Cave Springs 14 years ago.

"How did you happen to pick this spot to retire in?" I asked Mr. Egbert.

"Well, sir," he said, "I rode thru this gap in '94, looking for a lost mine. There was hardly even a trail here then.

"Many times after that I came up thru here. We always camped here because of the wonderful water in these springs. I liked this spot.

"Well, I had the flu in 1918, and I never really got over it. So in 1924 when the doctor told me I better go to the desert for good or I wouldn't live six months, I said 'Doc, I know exactly where to go.'

"We bought 10 acres here. We hauled lumber and everything for 60 miles in a Model-T, and started building. We've been building ever since."

– November 22, 1939

THOUGHTS IN A GRAVEYARD

TOMBSTONE, Ariz.—This is the place where they used to kill a man before breakfast every morning, and where the newspaper was (and still is) so aptly called The Epitaph.

It is the silver-mining town that blossomed and roared in the '80s. It is the home of the Bird Cage Theatre and Boothill Graveyard. From the reading I have done, I don't believe there was ever a tougher Western town than Tombstone.

But memory is kept well alive in Boothill Graveyard. It is on a knoll, just past the edge of town. The earth is hard, and only thorny little cactus growths are on the ground. From among the graves you can stand and look for countless miles. The wind blows hard, and the air is cool, for it is high and spaceless up there.

Many of Tombstone's notorious dead are buried there—five highwaymen who were lynched, a few who were legally hanged, some who were shot to death by Wyatt Earp and his deputies. Nobody has been buried here for more than 30 years. Except . . .

There is one new grave. A shoulder-high fence of yucca sticks surrounds it. The headstone is a lovely piece of petrified wood, set on a large rock. And on it is inscribed:

Quong Kee
1858-1938
A Friend to All
Rest in Peace

Quong Kee was an old Chinaman. He had lived in Tombstone almost since there was a Tombstone. He knew both the quick and the dead of those early days. He saw everything that ever happened to make Tombstone famous. And he just carried on being good to people.

He died last year. There was one man who felt it more than the others. He had been an orphan long ago in Tombstone, and Quong Kee fed him and helped him along. The man today is a well-to-do Arizona newspaper publisher, and he asked that Quong Kee be buried in Boothill. It was he who put up the tasteful monument.

Strange what the years do. Far, far away is China where Quong Kee came from. And far away, too, are the days of the bold killers of our old West. And the graveyard that was once a curse has now become an honored place.

You stand in Boothill among the thorny sage, and it all seems so great somehow, without your knowing why it was great. You simply know that these were wonderful days when killers walked upright instead of slinking, and you know you admire old Chinese people, and you know the desert is deadly and hideous and lovely, and it's a long way to the sky, and the wind tells better than anything else the helpless, futile passing of time.

Which doesn't make any sense to you, but it does to me.

It is interesting to watch the war-feeling in people's minds, as the miles go under our wheels and the weeks of the war wear on.

Traveling as we do from here to there we get, I suppose, what the chart-makers would call a cross-section. And this cross-section is about the most unanimous I've ever observed on any one subject.

It shows that in the West, when people speak about the war, they say mainly, "Oh to hell with it." But mainly they don't speak about it at all.

Letters from Washington and New York tell us that every gathering of friends these days practically ends in a fist fight over war dissensions. But we have recently spent entire evenings with whole roomfulls of people without the war even being mentioned once.

For a moment—a few weeks—there was a pause in everybody's life. We all lived in bewilderment of instability; no man knew what might be his lot a year from today.

But the climax didn't come; we peeked back around the corner, and nothing was there. There the sinews of people's hopes began to knit, and they picked up the solidity of future expectancy again, and now once more they think and plan on what they may do next year or the year after that.

People don't do that who are interested in war. Out here, we think the East is doing the rest of us no good with too much war blab-blab.

— November 28, 1939

ERNIE HAS ROUGH RIDE

ALAMAGORDO, N.M.—The White Sands of Alamagordo shine with a dazzling light. You must wear dark glasses or the tears will come to your squinty eyes and there will be nothing in your vision but glare.

There is nothing like the White Sands anywhere in the world. They are an albino Sahara. They are miles of drifted sugar. They are an ocean of utter white. They astound you and give you the creeps.

Out on the sands there is no sound, no perspective, no single thing to break the vast whiteness. The dunes rise and fall in graceful mounds, some as high as 10-story buildings. There are shadows that make a camera jump. There are dreams and mirages and food for the sober. And for the little people—the Sands look so good that children eat them.

These White Sands cover a strip about 30 miles long and 15 miles wide. What they are, really, is crystallized gypsum. They were made into a National Monument in 1933.

Next to Nature, I suppose Tom Charles is most responsible for the Sands. He has lived with them for 30 years. He loves them in the way one human loves another. His devotion is really what brought them into governmental status and public acclaim.

Mr. Charles has been the Government's custodian from the beginning, but a couple of months ago he faced retirement for age. He couldn't bear to leave the Sands, so he asked and was given the first and only concession within the Sands.

Mr. and Mrs. Charles drive the 20 miles from Alamagordo every day, way out into the heart of the Sands, out to a natural bowl sort of hidden away among the white dunes, and there they wait for the tourists.

He has a Plymouth sedan with big air-wheels. He takes tourists on a four-mile, 15-minute drive, for 25 cents apiece. He goes right up over the top of dunes, runs along the ridges, swoops down the slopes. It is like roller-coastering over clouds.

In his first month—an off month at that—he made 338 of these trips over the Sands with tourists. He thinks by next summer he'll need a couple of extra cars.

I went for a mild ride with Mr. Charles. And then Custodian Johnwill Faris wanted me to take a ride with him. He admitted later he kind of gave me the works.

Mr. Faris, it seems, read last spring about our trip down the rapids of the San Juan River. So he haid to himself, "If Ernie comes here we're going to give him a real ride."

And boy did he! He ran straight up the side of dunes, and wham down the other side. You can't see the other side till you're over the ridge, and it's too late. Sometimes the other side is almost straight up and down.

Mr. Faris didn't care. He soared over the top of ridges so sharp that our front wheels would just drop thru space till they hit the downward slope.

We charged down banks so steep we had to brace ourselves. We ran slopingly sideways along the banks of dunes, so Mr. Faris could show me you can't turn a car over out here.

It was the roughest ride I'd ever had. Mr. Faris got a big kick out of it. So did I. Sometimes my breath would go clear away. Oh, it was wonderful.

And after that we drove to another round bowl all closed in with white dunes, and there we had a picnic lunch and hot coffee. It tasted excruciatingly good, especially since I had thought I'd never live to see another meal.

The White Sands are phenomenal in a dozen ways. They are a desert, yet not a desert. For anywhere you can dig down a few inches with your hands and find water.

No janitor is needed for White Sands. Each morning the dunes are white and rippled and clean. All refuse is covered up. The wind does it.

Few people take long hiking trips across the Sands, for the walking is too hard. Tourists may drive their own cars over the dunes, but a lot of them get stuck. Mr. Charles doesn't charge anything to dig them out, but he should.

It would be easy to get lost on the Sands, because there aren't any landmarks anywhere. But people are so afraid they'll get lost that nobody does.

Only in winter, when the snow comes, is the vast uncanny whiteness broken by a little disillusionment. For then contrast is there, and to your surprise you see that the white sands are not really as white as the driven snow.

Only a little of the sand, right on top, dries out and blows. Consequently the dunes shift very slowly. The whole area is moving toward Alamagordo—20 miles away—at the rate of eight inches a year. Alamagordo won't have to blow its evacuation siren very soon.

Always the sands are cold. Just under the surface it is 56 degrees. In summer people come out by the hundreds, with blankets, and sleep away the sweltering nights.

They say sunset is the most wonderful time to see the Sands. But if you stay for that, you must then drive many miles after dark.

I think the day will come when the Goverment will allow a nice little white hotel to be built in one of the thousands of dune-surrounded cups. It is something necessary, and it wouldn't defile more than a pinpoint of the vast sands. Nature is all right, I always say, but there's nothing like an easy chair and a soft bed.

— December 8, 1939

In the past few years there has been building up within me an obsession that the only way to peace of mind is to go somewhere in the desert, far away from things, and just sit down.

. . . Ernie Pyle

PART TWO

THE LONELY LAND

Introduction
to
THE LONELY LAND
by
Ed Ainsworth

Loneliness was a part of his nature.

Ernie Pyle responded to beckoning vistas unspoiled by the presence of man, to the solitudes of desert and mountain, to the silent places where only Nature breathed and even she seemed to be holding her breath. A craving in his blood sent him at intervals to the most remote parts of the Southwest, as if only in the brooding quietness of red meas and tawny arroyos reaching for the horizon could he find the solace his spirit demanded.

Sometimes these quests for physical and mental regeneration at Nature's symbolic springs in the wilderness he encountered human beings who dwelt in isolation. Then, in his own way, Ernie Pyle sought from them the secrets of their life, why they had fled from civilization and turmoil to those more tranquil surroundings.

From them he extracted the essences of philosophy or religion which sustained them.

He became vicariously, a part of their existence. From them to him flowed the spiritual communion which always enabled him to judge people in so kindly a fashion and to translate to others, in words, the charm of their simple reasoning processes.

He understood. He transmitted. He transmuted.

So it was on all his trips to the great realm of upreared rock pinnacles, Joshua trees, barrel cactus, Sahuaros, and the pointed peaks of the jagged ranges.

After he established a home of his own in Albuquerque—called by Dr. Lawrence Clark Powell, the librarian and Southwestern scholar of the University of California at Los Angeles, "the heart of the heartland of the Southwest"—

Ernie Pyle was situated so he could penetrate easily to the remote regions which continually called him.

He ranged over New Mexico, Colorado, Utah, Nevada and Arizona, forever beguiled by promises of sojourns in quiet places.

And California beckoned him too.

He was intimately acquainted with parts of California which few men of his generation had seen. The awesome reaches of Death Valley and the Funeral Mountains lured him and so did the Mojave Desert and the Old Spanish Trail. He traveled from Ballarat to Earp and counted wild sheep along the Colorado.

Of necessity, he sometimes encountered human beings in these lonely places, too.

When he did he wrote their stories understandingly, always with an undercurrent as if he were saying, "Perhaps Ernie Pyle will linger here awhile with you."

But he never really lingered.

The next bend in the trail always lured him on. The next mountain needed to be climbed. The next arroyo had to be crossed.

In between, though, Ernie took time to sit for a little interval and wish he could stay longer.

His stories because of this are entwined in the fiber of the Lonely Land.

* * *

Ernie Pyle sensed in the 1930s that another war might might be coming The thought oppressed him. He sought to shake it off by going forth, almost like a knight errant, to seek the Holy Grail of peace and contentment in those parts of the nation where Nature still held sway, man was far away, and only God was near. Strangely enough, he found in some remote parts of burgeoning California, the nearest likeness to his fanciful and hoped-for land of loneliness. Despite emigrants swarming to its warmer clime in depression years, California retained in its far-away mountains many vestiges of primitive splendor and in its deserts some oases of quietness. Ernie Pyle sought these out from 1938 on into the war years of 1942, the period covered by the ensuing columns. These describe what he found.

—Ed Ainsworth

ERNIE VISITS CAVE SPRINGS

DEATH VALLEY, Calif.—In the past few years there has been building up within me an obsession that the only way to peace of mind is to go somewhere in the desert, far away from things, and just sit down.

In my saner moments I realize that wouldn't work for me at all. Yet it is a beguiling dream. I like to roll it around in my mind.

Hence, whenever I run onto people living an easy and apparently composed life in some remote corner I go poking around like a busybody, trying to find out just how they do it.

Seldom have I been more intrigued than by the mode of living of the two people who are the population of a place called Cave Springs, high in a bare mountain gap looking down upon Death Valley. They are Mrs. Ira Sweetman and her cousin, Adrian Egbert, and from all appearances they have things cinched.

They live in a three-room cottage and in half a dozen caves. There's nothing nutty about it. The caves are practical. And handmade. Mr. Egbert made them himself.

Mr. Egbert used to be a mining engineer, and he has had construction experience too. He knew how to construct a little kingdom out of the rock barrenness of Cave Springs to which he and Mrs. Sweetman came to live in 1924.

Their house is perched on a small bluff, alongside the trail. There is a good-sized living room, with big windows taking in the desert sun. And a kitchen, big like a farm kitchen. And back of the living room is one bedroom, which abuts the solid rock wall back of it. And now the caves—

One leads straight back from the kitchen door. In it are long shelves, stocked with canned goods, like a grocery store. They could live for months on this stock.

The next cave is a house within itself—two bedrooms in the back, and a sort of sitting room in front. Mr. Egbert sleeps here the year round. It never freezes in winter and seldom gets above 70 in summer, even tho it goes to 115 outside. A little shaft goes from the back bedroom up to the surface for ventilation. The rooms never get damp.

These rooms are furnished just like a house. The walls and ceiling are jagged rock, white-washed.

The next cave is a sort of workshop and office. And the next one contains the most important thing for life on the desert—water.

It seeps thru the rock and drips into a tub. Mr. Egbert says it is the most perfect water in the world; he has had it tested. Under foot, covered with flooring, is a five-barrel tank, in case of emergency. There has never been an emergency.

The next cave is a garage, where Mrs. Sweetman keeps her new golden-brown Dodge coupe. Mr. Egbert's old Model-T sits out in the open.

There are still other caves and semi-caves. They house little chicken lots, and various machinery, and a little cabin for friends who might come to visit.

It took Mr. Egbert years to make three caves. He did it by drilling, and blasting with dynamite, as in a gold mine.

Their days have no set schedule. There is an old alarm clock in the kitchen, but the alarm has never been set.

Mrs. Sweetman's gray hair is bobbed and she is smiling and enthusiastic. She drives 60 miles to Barstow about once a week for mail, 150 to San Bernardino twice a month for supplies, and occasionally on into Los Angeles. She always puts her evening gown and slippers in the back of the car, in case she is invited to a formal party. She's leaving in a few days on a three-month cruise to Central America.

Mr. Egbert hasn't been to town for three years. Just doesn't want to go. And yet he is delighted when anybody drops past.

He is a great reader. He uses a pair of glasses that cost 60 cents. He subscribes to about 10 magazines—Time, Life, Literary Digest, National Geographic, Reader's Digest, Desert Magazine, a mining magazine.

He has a big radio, with two storage batteries to run it. Outside is a little windmill on a tripod, generating power for the batteries.

They burn oil in the cookstove, for their isn't enough wood within 50 miles to start a Boy Scout fire.

They own 10 acres of ground around the house, and 100 acres off over the hill. There are old mine shafts all around, but nothing much has ever come out of them.

The only thing they raise is a few chickens. But that's hard too, for the bobcats keep breaking in. Coyotes don't bother, and there are hardly any rattlesnakes. There are wild mountain sheep in the vicinity.

"But you're not allowed to shoot them, it's against the law," I said.

"Well, I won't let one come up and bite me," Mr. Egbert said. "Three or four have tried!"

Mr. Egbert says they can live on about $40 a month. He must mean just groceries, for that couldn't include the new car, and gasoline, and all the magazines. But anyway, they don't have to worry or scratch. "We made our stake before we ever came up here," says Mr. Egbert.

— March 23, 1938

FLOOD DAMAGE VIEWED

VICTORVILLE, Calif.—We who sat in our Hollywood apartments during the Big Rain of 1938, and watched the downpour from a fifth-story window and read the papers twice a day, never realized how bad the California flood really was.

It wasn't until today, more than two weeks after the big burst, when we started out into the world again, that we saw first-hand what a California flood can do.

We drove east from Los Angeles to San Bernardino—75 miles. The road was easily passable, altho they were still scraping mud from it in places.

At San Bernardino we turned north to cross the mountains thru Cajon Pass. They told us the road was all right, so we went on. Everything seemed fine, and we hummed along the pavement, flood all behind us. We thought.

Suddenly we came over the brow of a hill. There was some kind of activity ahead. A motorcycle cop in yellow slicker and rain hat waved us down.

"Straddle the center line, and put your bumper against the car ahead of you," he said. "You can go thru at 3 o'clock." It was then a few minutes after 1 p.m.

So we bumped the car ahead. And in a minute another car bumped us behind. And there we were wedged in tight, in a line that eventually grew to more than 100 automobiles.

The cops were swell. They explained that the road really wasn't bad ahead, but there were lots of slides to be cleared, and if they let traffic keep flowing the steam shovels wouldn't get anything done. So traffic went thru every two hours. The cops joked with the people, and answered silly questions, and were good-natured about everything.

An hour and a half is a long time to wait. So I got out my book on the life of "Lucky" Baldwin and went at it. It was the first time in weeks I'd had time to read a book.

But the people from other cars kept walking up and down, and I never can keep from looking at people, so the result was I read one page 40 times and will have to read it again some day to find out what it said.

An ice-cream man had seized opportunity by the tail and was out there in his little white truck doing a land-office business.

Which is proof that the American people don't know what to do with themselves. Here they had an hour and a half to kill, and the only way they could think of to kill it was by eating ice cream—on a day so cold and miserable that the very thought of getting out of the car threw me into a nervous chill.

But time passed, and the people ate all the ice cream, and one guy with a truckload of oranges started selling them. Finally 3 o'clock came, and the cops were as good as their word. Right on the dot they pulled aside the barriers and waved us ahead.

Special privilege was given to six huge busses, which belonged to the railroads and were carrying rail passengers 150 miles from Los Angeles to a temporary terminal on the desert. The busses pulled around and went thru fast.

The "controlled" section of the road was 15 miles long. Across the gulch we could see long stringers of railroad track, sagging like twine, without any foundation. We could see track hanging from bridges. And some bridges completely out.

The small store and filling station that we remembered were crumpled and more than half buried. Roofs of tourist cabins back behind stuck stupidly up a foot above the earth.

The avalanche which filled a valley and covered the highway for blocks was all dry now, and solid, and permanent looking. To make a new highway path thru it was just like digging a canal.

Six steam shovels were working in one spot, uncovering the railroad. The bulldozers and shovels had already cut a canyon for us, and it was like driving thru a roofless tunnel.

Surely it will take months to get this little area, of maybe half a square mile, back into what it was before a few hours of water came.

What we saw in this day of driving, they say, was simply nothing compared to other places. But it was a sight to us who, like 99 of every 100 people in Los Angeles, knew no more of the flood than getting our ignition drowned out, sloshing to the store in the rain and doing without lights for a couple of hours.

– March 18, 1938

BARSTOW MEN SPROUT SPINACH

BARSTOW, Calif.—People look funny in Barstow.

The hotel clerk looked as if he'd been on a two-day jag. The bellboy, in red Spanish trousers and wide leather sash, resembled Morgan the Pirate.

The state motorcycle cop looked as tho he had been on flood duty for 72 hours straight. The editor of the local weekly appeared to have just come in after riding the rods from Omaha. Even the barber had forgot to shave.

Curiosity at last got the better of me, so I asked somebody about it. And then it was all made clear. The whisker season had started in Barstow.

It opened officially on March 1, A few citizens jumped the gun, and by now have immense forests on their faces. One grocery clerk had a wild brown bush with two coal-black tufts at each side of his chin, like tusks.

The Van Dyke seems to be leading by about three-to-one. The hideous Mexican sideburn is a runner-up. Now and then you see an Irish muttonchop. And a few of the more arrogant are just letting them grow in all directions at once.

The cause behind the effect is Barstow's celebration of Calico Days on May 14 and 15.

Here at Barstow we are in the heart of the great Mojave Desert—a barren, mountainous country, dry, snaky, full of frontier lore, the lore of the 20-muleteam borax drivers, the lore of prospectors on burros and of the shafts from which came silver.

The mountains hereabout are called the Calico mountains, because when it rains they look like calico, with all the colors of the spectrum. About 12 miles from Barstow, up a steep canyon, are the remains of the Calico silver mine and the old boom camp of Calico. They took $15,000,000 from this mine.

But that was long ago. Calico, once 3000, now is only a few old adobe houses. Barstow is the metropolis—even tho it has only 600 people. It has a Chamber of Commerce and a Kiwanis Club. It has an exclusive desert inn. It advertises its cool summer nights and its bracing winter air, rather than assay value of its ore and the immensity of its borax loads.

And out of the haze that is the past, it is trying to recapture once a year the flavor of the old days. Of course, it can't be done, but at least an exhibition can be made. And whisker-growing is part of the show.

The Calico Days celebration is new. This is only the second one. They tried it first in 1935, and it was successful. But the committee members quarreled over bringing in Los Angeles leg shows for a frontier celebration—so they dropped it in '36 and '37.

This year they are starting in earnest on a permanent basis, and in a few years the Calico Days celebration may be a tradition in itself, as well-known as the Pendleton Roundup or the Hopi Snake Dance.

The center of the to-do this year will be on the desert, just east of town. They'll have all ginds of gambling halls and other concessions. You can play faro bank or roulette. It's against the California law—but for two days the law just comes and looks and sees nothing: "Anything goes but murder," they say.

At the end of the "street" of concessions will be a rodeo ring. The local cowboys and cowgirls will perform, and at night there will be professional entertainment which may be anything from toe-dancers to a three-ring circus.

On the Calico Days grounds is an old jail, hauled down from one of the dead mining camps. It is authentic, and has actually held train robbers and two-gun men.

The grounds will be patrolled by a "sheriff" and his deputies, and any man without a beard will be arrested. By paying a 50-cent fine he may go on about his business; if he demands a jury trial he'll get it, and probably wind up in jail.

On the final night all the beards for miles around will be herded into the rodeo arena and paraded around and around, like cattle. A jury will select the finest.

The men of Barstow are going in wholeheartedly for the beard idea. Nearly every one in town who can sprout a beard at all has one under way.

I asked a fellow what the women of Barstow thought about the beard business. "Well, they don't like it," he said, "but they have to put up with it."

And as time goes on, Barstow will look even funnier. A few weeks before the actual celebration, many of Barstow's residents will begin dressing as the men of the '80s did. They'll go about their usual business in the odd costume of broad miner's hat, checkered shirt, overalls, square-heeled boots, and carrying an old gun.

Many a spring tourist driving thru here is due for a fright, unless he happens to have been a regular reader of this column. This colum prepares all kinds of people for all kinds of things, including whisker-fright. Subscribe today.

— March 19, 1938

"LATE" FRED SAMPSON

BARSTOW, Calif.—Fred Sampson is 61, and he never knew until three years ago that had this power over little animals.

Sampson can sit down in the desert, and in a few hours have chipmunks crawling all over him. "They don't know I'm a man," he says. "They think I'm just a big chipmunk."

He can scare up a wild jackrabbit and the rabbit will come back and eat out of his hand. He keeps skunks in his cabin, and has never been "sprayed." Mice and pack rats are among his favorite companions.

Sampson is not an eccentric. He is merely a man with an artistic side to his soul, who has been over the hurdles and wound up, with considerable composure, in the vast desert.

He was born in Iowa of a school teacher father, and raised on a farm in Arkanasa. But his career has been mainly as an artist. He studied and taught at the Chicago Art Institute for 10 years.

He has worked in powder factories, been an aerial photographer, served in the Army. He has run an art school in Detroit, and painted sketches for the movies in Hollywood. It was when the movie work ran out that he came to the desert.

"I was born two weeks late," he says, "And I've been late ever since." He didn't begin studying art until he was 30. He was 40 when he went to war. He was 50 when he tried to crash Hollywood. He was 55 when he came to the desert.

He loves the desert. He never gets lonesome. He likes the silence, and the space, and likes to sit alone and think. Always being late has given him a quality of mental calm, for it showed him there's no use to go rushing about.

"I'm content now because so many desires are behind me," he says. "I've passed the point where I feel the need to create a home and family. I've given up the idea of becoming a great artist. I don't have to try to make a lot of money any more."

But of course a man has to have something to do. And now, past 60, Sampson has just discovered a work which he feels will give him both a living and a sense of achievement. That work is photographing the little animals of the desert.

His photographs are truly remarkable. His chipmunks look like men! His rabbits are as winsome as babies. He achieves this, he says, because of his harmony with animals.

His little animals aren't really pets. They come to his cabin, and stay a

while, and go away. None is trained to do tricks for the camera. Sampson just plays around with them out on the rocks, and now and then he snaps a picture.

He talks all the time he's working with the animals. That's to let them know he isn't going to hurt them. He knows they can't understand English, but they can understand him.

For example, when he says "Look out now, I'm going to move," they just go on playing and don't pay any attention when he moves among them.

But when he says "Look out, the skunk is coming and he'll get you," the chipmunks made one grand scram for the nearest holes.

"When I take a picture," Sampson says, " I take it with their full consent and knowledge. Most wild-animal pictures are taken by stealth, or setting some kind of trigger to trip a hidden camera. But my pictures are taken with the full co-operation of the animals."

He says the whole thing is based on the fact that he never tells a lie to an animal. He never tricks them, or goes back on his word. Also, he feeds them 2400 pounds of grain a year, which may have some bearing on the matter.

Chipmunk and rabbit pictures sell the best. People don't care for skunk pictures. That's too bad, for Sampson's skunks are fine. He had one skunk that would get on his bed and paw at his bare feet, then run up and look in his face to see if he had awakened.

When he's alone at his cabin Sampson goes naked most of the time. He says it's so hot in summer you almost have to. And then also, the sun cured him of T.B. Today he is hale and hearty, and looks much younger than his years. He has never smoked, drunk, nor got married, but doesn't mind other people doing those things.

Sampson is well informed on geology and metallurgy. He owns some land, and says there's gold in his hills.

Sampson believes in the unconscious tranference of messages between minds. He says he can easily find things that people hid in a room, and tell what other people are thinking.

I really believe there is some basis for his belief. But it doesn't work on his animals—at least I can't work it.

While I sat talking with Sampson, one of his pet cats lay curled up on my lap. I don't like cats, so I sent this animal a thought message to get the hell off of there. But I just don't seem to have the knack, for the cat never even woke up. I expect if I told a chipmunk to go way, the beast would turn and bite my arm off.

— March 21, 1938

ERNIE SEES DEATH VALLEY

DEATH VALLEY, Calif.—California's recent floods extended clear back into the barren wastes of the Mojave Desert. And it was the circumstance of the floods which plunged us into one of the most spectacular panoramas that I have ever looked upon.

I refer to the descent into Death Valley from the south end. I don't suppose one tourist in 5000 ever sees Death Valley from this angle. Or for that matter, ever gets into the south half of the valley at all.

We didn't make this approach thru superior wisdom. It was simply that the main paved highways were washed out, and it was a case of come in thru the Cave Springs dirt road or not at all.

You're on the rim of Death Valley at Cave Springs. From there you drop 3600 feet in a twisty, bumpy, 15-mile drive onto the floor of the valley. Every foot of the way is an appalling spectacle of desolation, upheaval, distance, and a silent, almost spectral, beauty.

One thing I wanted to find out about Death Valley was whether it is actually a place that is limited, circumscribed, measurable—or whether it just spraddles all over everywhere without any real sides. I figured you couldn't really stand and see Death Valley.

Well, you can. It is limited. It is definite. It is like an immense slash in the earth. It has a floor, and high sides. It is 130 miles long and ranges from 6 to 14 miles wide.

You can't see from one end to the other, because it is too far, and anyway it makes a turn. But there's no place in the valley where you can't look up and see the high, bare mountains hemming you in.

There is nothing consistent about the valley floor. I have driven the whole 130 miles, and there is hardly a five-mile stretch that is the same.

Some places it is sand. Some places actually swampy and marshy. Some places hard and black, like old lava. Some places snow white, salt beds, the same as in Utah.

In some places there is no vegetation whatever. But most of the valley has a thin scattering of low shrubs—greasewood, bunch grass, small mesquite, and even some flowers. There is almost no cactus.

When we came down into the valley the rough gravel road ran northward for miles and miles, right out in the center of the valley, as straight as a ruler.

We had to cross the Armagosa River, which flows (sometimes) down the valley's center. The river bed is flat and usually dry. You just drive across it. If there's much water, then the river is wide and you don't cross at all.

Before you get midway up the valley, the salt marshes set in. Then the road swings away from them, over against the foot of the mountains, and becomes very winding.

That famous "lowest point in the United States" is not in the center of the valley, but clear over to one side. It's only a few feet from the road, and you could go stand in it if you wanted to wade in the salt marsh. I just looked at the sign and let it go at that.

It's 280 feet below sea level. If you built a 20-story building there, its spire would still be lower than a rowboat on San Francisco Bay.

We wondered if we'd feel as if we needed to go into a decompression tank, like deep sea divers, when we started up into the altitudes again. But we didn't feel funny, either at 280 below or back up to 4000.

You've all heard of Death Valley's terrific summer heat. Well, from what I've been able to pick up, everything is true—and then some. It has been officially recorded as high as 134 in the shade—and there is no shade, except artificial shade.

I would be afraid to drive down into Death Valley in summer. Every summer, even in this modern day, somebody is lost. A prospector, who should know better; or a tourist, who leaves the road against advice, gets stuck in the sand, and it's good-by.

They say that often you can't see 100 yards for the heat waves. Walking far is fatal. Changing a tire is dangerous. Just lifting a jug is exertion.

As far as I can learn, there is not a single year-round private home in Death Valley. There are, however, two spots of lavish comfort for winter dwellers. One is the Stovepipe Wells Hotel on the west side of the vally. The other is Furnace Creek, on the east side.

At Furnace Creek there is a magnificent desert inn, a dude ranch and the headquarters of Death Valley National Monument.

But civilization in Death Valley locks its doors on May 1. The hotels close. Three or four people stay at Furnace Creek. A lone watchman at Stovepipe Wells. The Indians of the southern end take to the mountains. If you wander across Death Valley in July and die, you'll die alone.

— March 24, 1938

PYLE DISCOVERS BORAX

DEATH VALLEY, Calif.—I cannot remember a time in my childhood when there was not a box of 20-Mule-Team Borax in our kitchen cabinet at home.

But thru all these years my knowledge of borax never developed one whit beyond the fact that we had a box in the kitchen. I never knew what borax was, where it came from, or what it was for, outside of softening water.

But now I know. It has a hundred uses. It is a rather rare product, and most of the world's supply is in these deserts. The history of Death Valley is almost the history of borax. Let's go way back!

There were some small borax workings in Nevada prior to 1880. But in that year a propsector named Aaron Winters discovered borax on the floor of Death Valley. He sold his claims for $20,000.

William T. Coleman bought these claims and worked borax out of Death Valley until 1889. Then he was taken over by the Pacific Coast Borax Co., which is still the biggest borax company in the world.

Borax, like gold, is mined in two ways—on the surface, and in hard-rock shaft mines. The borax company built great mills right here in the valley, and did its own refining. But it had to get this borax to market, and it was 165 miles to a railroad. Out of this dire need came the 20-mule-team borax wagons.

It became a transportation service as daring, as romantic and as thrilling in its way as the pony express or the overland stage.

These great borax loads were hauled over utter desert from Death Valley to Mojave, Calif. The wagons were immense. A 20-mule team always pulled two wagons and a trailer with water and hay. The load was often as much as 40,000 pounds of borax, plus 16,000 pounds of wagons and water. Think of it—28 tons, nearly a ton and a half per mule, up mountain grades and over parching sands!

Each wagon carried a driver and a "swamper." The driver used a 22-foot blacksnake whip, plus plenty of rocks and usswords. The lead mules were 120 feet from the driver's seat. They say that a borax wagon driver had to be even more skillful, and tougher, than a stagecoach driver.

The wagons made about 16 miles a day—10 days for the trip to Mojave. There were 10 stations, each supplied with water, for overnight stops.

They didn't go in dead summer. But even so, the heat was so terrific that men's nerves went to pieces. They couldn't keep the same driver and swamper together for many trips.

Early in the century they started experimenting with tractors, and then in 1915 a railroad was built into the borax mill in Death Valley.

So there hasn't been a 20-mule borax team for at least 25 years. But they still use the trade mark, because it is a good one. Two of the old drivers are left. One lives in San Bernardino and the other still works for the borax company as a carpenter at Death Valley Junction.

Two items in my borax lesson surprised me. One is that they haven't mined a grain of borax in Death Valley for more than 10 years. And the other is that the concern which does most of the borax mining—the famous 20-mule-team concern—is a British company.

In 1927 borax was discovered near Cramer, Calif., on the Mojave Desert. It was a much purer borax than the stuff up here. And it was practically on top of a main-line railroad. So they just shut down here and moved to Cramer.

There is enough borax around Cramer to last 50 years or more. But when and if that runs out, the Death Valley borax will still be here.

Now about that British company. The parent office is in London, and it has potash holdings all over the world. But they say there isn't an Englishman in the whole outfit over here.

The company—the Pacific Coast Borax Co.—mines two-thirds of the borax used in the world today. Half of its output is exported.

Most of it is shipped out in bulk, in sacks. The only borax you and I ever heard of was the box on the kitchen shelf, but they say this "package business" is such a small part of the whole that it's almost a joke.

And what do they use borax for, besides softening water? Well, in a general way, borax has the quality of taking out impurities. Borax is what makes glass so clear. Borax is what makes enamel so smooth. Borax is what welders sprinkle on two pieces of hot steel before putting them together. Borax is what the dentist stirs into his little cup of gold before filling your tooth. Borax is used to purify paint and clean mechanics' hands.

And the borax company is now working (with an eye in my direction) on a compound designed to purify men's souls.

— March 25, 1938

ROUGH ROAD TO SCOTTY'S CASTLE

DEATH VALLEY, Calif.—The sign said "Road Closed." We sat and looked at it for a long time. Finally a truck came thru, and we waved it down.

"Is it absolutely impossible to get thru to Scotty's castle?" I asked the driver.

He said: "Well, two cars started thru day before yesterday. They must have got thru, for we haven't heard from them. But they say the washouts are pretty bad."

I told the driver I couldn't bear the thought of being within 25 miles of Scotty's famous place and not getting up there to write a piece about him.

"Well," the driver said, "if I was you I'd tackle it. Be careful not to straddle any big rocks, and don't get hung up on the bottom."

"If we shouldn't get there in time to come back before dark, is there any place around there to stay?" I asked.

"No," he said.

"But Scotty has plenty of room, and he'll probably put you up. He has taken in paying guests in a pinch. Why don't you go on and try it? The road is good till you get within 16 miles of there."

So we started over the "closed" road, on to Death Valley Scotty's. It was a gravel road, and altho it lay on the open floor of the broad valley it had been terribly washed out by the recent floods that came raging out of the mountains.

When we figured we were within 16 miles I said:

"Now let's time ourselves, so we'll know how long before dark we'll have to start back. It's just 1 o'clock now."

And I said further: "No matter how bad it is, we can surely make 16 miles in an hour and a half." Such is the sublime confidence of fools.

We were an hour going the first three miles. We were three hours going the next ten feet. After that, nothing mattered much anyhow.

I built that road with my own hands for three miles. I heaved rocks, dug rocks, carried rocks. I filled up great chasms, and knocked off humps. I built grades, and causeways, and dikes, and roadbeds, not to mention a right-of-way or two.

Inch by inch we progressed over those three miles. In a couple of dozen places the road was simply washed away and you faced a rock-strewn gulch. If I'd had any sense I would have turned back. But greenhorns driving in Death Valley don't have any sense. That's why so many of them are dead.

It was a stiff up-pull all the way. The day was warm. The radiator and

I boiled alternately. While it cooled, I built roads. By the time the car was cool, I'd be boiling over.

Like all good desert travelers we had no shovels, no extra oil, and exactly one pint of water for the radiator and me. I drank the water and threw the bottle at the radiator.

Finally we accomplished the three miles. And then we came to something you could distinguish from the Grand Canyon only by the fact that it was in California instead of Arizona. This wasn't a washout, it was a cataclysm.

My construction work here consumed nearly half an hour. Finally hot and weary under Death Valley's March sun, I stood back and inspected my engineering accomplishments.

I studied, surveyed, arrived at a decision. "If I can just keep the car moving," I said "I think we can make it across." The effort of making that remark took almost the last of my waning strength.

We unloaded every bit of our voluminous baggage. We dug with our hands, and with wrench handles. We ruined our clothes. We spun the tires till they smoked. We got the motor so hot it would barely run. We jacked up the back end so the gear box would clear a rock, and that left no traction for the wheels.

The thing was hopeless, and permanent. The sun dropped behind the Panamint Range. It looked like a night under the stars in Death Valley.

It was 12 miles to Scotty's place, all uphill, and it would take me at least four hours to walk it. Maybe even longer. I wasn't sure that I ought to start, without any drinking water.

And then suddenly we were aware that two cars had come out of nowhere and pulled up at the brink of the washout, behind us. Some men got out, but I refused to speak to them, for I knew they were optical illusions and I have no truck with desert mirages.

But mirages or not, the men pushed, and dug, and threw rocks under the wheels, and pushed some more, and in a little while we were out. But the example was enough for them. They turned around and started back to Los Angeles—400 miles away.

And so finally, late in the afternoon, we reached our goal. Oily, dusty, sweaty, bleeding and weary—we pulled up in front of Death Valley Scotty's fabulous desert castle. A Filipino houseboy came out.

"Is Scotty around?" I asked.

The boy replied: "No, Scotty's in Los Angeles. He won't be back for a week!"

— March 26, 1938

TOO EXPENSIVE FOR ERNIE

SCOTTY'S CASTLE, Death Valley, Calif.– So Scotty's in Los Angeles, and won't be back for a week! Isn't that just dandy, after me wallowing a whole afternoon in Death Valley washouts to get up here.

It's too late to go back over that same road. I wouldn't tackle it after dark for any money. So I say to Walter, a cowboy who has charge while Scotty is away:

"Can you put us up for the night?" We would expect to pay, of course."

"Sure," says Walter, "we'll put you up for $40 apiece."

I don't say anything. I guess Walter thinks I'm going to pass out on him; for he goes on quickly:

"We had to put the price up so high to keep people from staying. Last year so many people stayed that the hotels down in the valley got to raising hell."

"So you won't let us stay all night then?"

"For $40 apiece," says Walter. He was serious.

"I can't pay $80, and wouldn't if I could. And I'm not going back over that road. Where can we stay?"

"Well, there's a dirt road into Nevada that isn't so bad," Walter says. "It's 27 miles to pavement, and 60 miles to Beatty. There's a good hotel there."

"O.K.," I said. "At least now that we're here we can go thru the castle, can't we?"

"It'll cost you $1.10 apiece," says Walter.

"O.K.," says I. "Let's go."

Walter took us thru the castle, but I'll wait till tomorrow to tell you about that. Today I want to give you my impression (as the impersonators say) of the reasons behind this $2,000,000 castle stuck out here in the desert sands.

The public-at-large believes that Scotty is an eccentric desert rat who has some mysterious and unlimited source of money.

Actually, people tell me, Scotty isn't eccentric at all. Most everybody in this sparsely settled desert knows him. They say he's a good fellow who's got a good thing, and they don't begrudge it.

Scotty's money actually comes from a man named Albert M. Johnson. As I get it, Johnson was in the West years ago, in a bad way with tuberculosis. Scotty met him and invited him out to his desert shack, saying it would cure Johnson's tuberculosis.

Well, Johnson came and stayed a few months, and did become a new man. He returned to Chicago and became wealthy.

Altho that story is known, it is usually accompanied by hazy concoctions about Johnson's fanatical gratitude to Scotty, how he has poured all this money into a castle for Scotty, and how Scotty has always refused to say where the money came from.

My impression is that there's no mystery about it all. I believe Johnson built the castle for himself, not for Scotty.

The Johnsons don't live in Chicago any more. They live in Los Angeles, one day's drive from here. Both Johnson and Mrs. Johnson spend a great deal of time up here. They have their regular rooms in the castle. Their wardrobes are stocked. Their private pictures are all over the place. Mr. Johson's chauffeur is a brother of Walter, the cowboy.

The castle was largely designed by Mrs. Johnson. It was furnished to her tastes. The ranch crest is J-S (Johnson-Scott) in a circle, and it's on practically everything. It's on dishes, and on tables, and on window hangings, and even on every fence post.

It is my impression that this castle belongs to Johnson, and that Scotty is a fellow who happens to be a good friend and just lives here, and probably gets plenty of spending money.

Somehow I had it in my head that this castle was started way back in the early 1900s. But actually it wasn't started until 1926. They built for six years, and then stopped.

The castle itself is finished. And all the fine outbuildings. But the great crooked swimming pool (the biggest one I've ever seen) lies unfinished.

Walter, the cowboy, says they quit building because they discovered some hitch about absolute title to the land. Six years have passed now, and Walter says they've sort of lost interest in doing anything more.

But in a little Mojave Valley town, at a lunch counter one night, I heard an old desert rat say they stopped because Johnson lost 45 million dollars in the depression.

Just a couple of years ago they started letting sightseers in. Last year 7000 people went thru the castle. That means $7000. Walter says they lost money on it, because of the added expense. But when we pinned Walter down, he couldn't think of any extra expense except the salary of a guide.

– March 28, 1939

TOURING SCOTTY'S CASTLE

SCOTTY'S CASTLE, Death Valley, Calif.—Death Valley Scotty's castle is just as elegant as you've always heard it was. And the surprising thing to me is that it's all in good taste. There's a warmness about it inside. It's a place you could live in.

The castle is not actually in Death Valley. It is back up a wide canyon, four miles from the valley proper. Why they picked this spot I have no idea. The canyon looks bedraggled, second-rate. The hills are puny. The earth has that black-streaked, washed-out appearance of West Virginia coal country (minus trees) .

The castle itself is not really immense. It has no great marble stairways, or vast ballrooms. You wouldn't get lost in it.

There is a sort of triple theme running thru the house—Spanish-Italian for one; desert life for two and just plain house for three. Oddly enough, they don't clash.

There are lots of other buildings. A powerhouse, built like a county courthouse, with a big clock face in each of the steeple's four sides. And a long, fine-looking building which Walter said was the "guest house." It's my private opinion that Scotty and the Johnsons live in this "guest house." I don't see how they could live in the castle with 7000 people walking thru it every year.

And there are stables, and a house for employes, and a big garage and machine shop, and a big glass mechanism on the hillside where water is heated by the sun.

The castle has a staff of six people—Walter, (the head man,) a guide, a bald-headed Chinese cook, a Filipino houseboy, and a couple of roustabouts.

Walter, the cowboy, took us thru the castle. Walter isn't the regular guide, but he knows the spiel. A new man, who has come up from Los Angeles to be the guide, went along to learn the ropes.

Walter wasn't a bad fellow at all. He got tickled at his own wisecracks. He had a sort of perpetual cat-ate-mouse smirk that indicated he thought he knew the whole business—visitors, castle and even himself—was sillier than hell.

First we had to put on flannel slippers over our shoes. Then we went into Scotty's bedroom—a corner room just off the living room.

Walter showed us a little hole in the wall, with a slide over it. You could stick a shotgun in there and fire it, and the shot would richochet at right angles and shoot past the window.

"That's in case Scotty's wife ever comes around," Walter laughed. (She lives in Reno, and they've had bitter divorce troubles.)

On the walls are pictures of Scotty when he was with Buffalo Bill's show. And other pictures, including his son, who is 23 now and in the Navy.

Then we went upstairs into Mrs. Johnson's room. She has a low, built-in bed, right against the wall. Walter showed us how she could swing out an iron bar, pull down a panel on hinges from the wall, let it rest on the bar, and have her breakfast in bed.

The main living room is two stories high, and a balcony runs clear around it. The great beams of the ceiling were carved right on the place, and they are the most beautiful and intricate ceiling beams I've ever seen.

We went thru the library (Walter opened small double doors above the fireplace mantel, and there were tinted pitcures of Scotty and Mr. Johnson, side by side.)

We went in to the sun parlor, or solarium, as Walter said. There was a sort of fountain there, with a background painted to represent the bottom of the ocean, and two big enamelled bullfrogs.

We went into the dining room, which is really magnificent. The walls are stocked with more beautiful dishes than you ever saw outside of a store, every one with the J-S crest on it.

We went into the big kitchen. "In that corner is a Spanish well," Walter said, "where we keep the garbage can and mops. It's genuine Spanish tile, too." (He smirked.)

Finally we crossed the second-story catwalk, took a wink at three or four beautifully furnished "overnight rooms," as Walter called them ($80, hah!), and wound up in the big music room.

This was the only place that looked like a museum. Some of the antique chairs had ribbon tied across so you couldn't sit down. On one side was a big cold fireplace, on the other side a dark little stage. In one corner was a pipe organ, hidden by a screen.

"You can play this either as a piano, a pipe organ, or by mechanical rolls," Walter said. "Would you like to hear one?"

We said yes, so Walter put on a roll, and the noise was so loud you could hardly talk. When that finished Walter put on another roll. We listened that one thru, and then he asked if we didn't want to hear another one. We said no, but he seemed to want to keep on playing.

Then we asked if that was the end of the tour, and he said yes.

— March 29, 1938

SHE STARTED SOMETHING

PALM SPRINGS, Calif.—Mother Coffman had no idea what she was starting. She couldn't possibly have visualized it all. Nobody could have.

But when Mother Coffman opened her little "boarding house" way back in 1909 in this seedy, sandy little village, unheard of at the time, she started what was to become the whole vast vogue of desert-vacationing.

All the great resorts of the desert—Tucson and Phoenix and Death Valley—the fancy hotels and the Southwest dude ranches and the thousands in trailers who have discovered the uncanny lure of the desert—it all began with Mother Coffman 33 years ago.

The whole thing was built on one woman's spiritual love for the desert. The desert has repaid her vastly for her affection. And she, in turn, still clings to the desert with a loyalty and a love that have never dimmed.

Few people know where the credit should go for revealing the desert to so many thousands, or how well the cloak of accomplishment is worn by the woman who did it. So I have come to Palm Springs to write about her—a pioneer woman, a remarkable woman.

Palm Springs now is world famous. There is a glamor about the very name. It is the ultimate in sun-vacationing. The movie world has made it doubly famous by adopting it.

In the beginning, Palm Springs was only for those quiet people who gained an elevation of spirit from the space and solitude of the empty sand. It was a retreat then.

Now it has grown into a resort of gaiety and ultra shops and great luxury—altho it is still essentially a retreat. If that's what you want.

There are many places to stay in Palm Springs. Nearly all of them are nice, and not all of them are expensive. You can pay anything from $4 a day on up. Some places are gay and clubbish; some are outdoorsy and cowboyish; some are trailerish and tourist-campy; and some are spacious and unspeakably luxurious and rich with an old dignity.

Of the latter, the Desert Inn stands at the top. The Inn has held its place thru three decades of changing taste in the desert vogue. There are hundreds of very rich people from all over America who wouldn't think of going anywhere here except the Desert Inn. And the Desert Inn is owned by Mrs. Nellie Coffman and her two sons.

The Inn is not built on the hotel plan—one big building. Instead, it is 35 acres of spacious loveliness. The guests live in rooms or suites or cottages thruout the grounds. There is nothing on the place higher than a story and a half. Once inside the grounds, it is as tho you had entered a quiet, private world. No one can tread on you.

A couple can't stay here for less than $20 a day. Most of them pay more than that, up to $40 and over. Movie queens must cover their lovely figures with something more than shorts or halters or they don't get into the dining room. Autos aren't allowed inside the grounds, except to unload baggage. A maid turns down your bed while you are at dinner. The place isn't snooty; it's just quietly dignified.

I came here purposely to write of Mrs. Coffman. But when I saw the lavishness of what she had created, saw the old and accepted wealth of the guest, saw the stability of the place, I was seized with a sudden stage fright.

And then when I finally did meet her, it seemed that she might have come from a Mid-West farm only yesterday. Her walk, her manner of dress, her direct and honest speech, her smalltown friendliness—they were as midwestern as clover hay.

And above all, she wasn't in any hurry. That's the trouble with most important people, they always have to run and do something else. But Mother Coffman is in no hurry.

A woman has to have character to start from nothing and fight her way up into the millionaire class. But she has to have even more character to prevent success from closing in on her, making her a spiritual hermit.

Nellie Coffman's years of success have put no guard rail around her at all. She is wise, but not sophisticated. Everybody is welcome to her thoughts, and she welcomes other people's. She is just herself.

"I've never had a monotonous day in my life," she says. That tells a lot about a person.

— March 25, 1942

RICHES THE HARD WAY

PALM SPRINGS, Calif.—Life really began after 40 for Nellie Coffman, the extraordinary woman who owns the Desert Inn here, and who is the founder of the entire institution of desert vacationing.

She is almost 75 now. She was 42 when she came to Palm Springs. She was a mature woman then, twice married, mother of two grown sons. She brought with her to Palm Springs a fanatical love for the desert, a complete lack of business experience, and a laughably small amount of money.

At the end of her first season as a resort proprietor she had $65 in the bank. She paid $50 of that on some land. She had to get thru the fall and start of her second season on $15. That was in 1909. Today you couldn't buy her out for two million.

But let's go back to the beginning.

Like practically all important people (ahem), Mrs. Coffman sprang from Indiana. She was born in the village of Pakota, on the banks of the Wabash. But she remembers little about it, for her folks moved to Texas when she was a child.

Her father was a contractor. Nellie Orr, as she was then, was brought up in Dallas. She married and had one son—George Roberson. Her first husband died. Later in California she married again and bore another son—Earl Coffman. Both are here with her today.

The history of the Orr family had been one of moving onward to new lands where there was more room. Theirs was the blood of pioneers. Down thru the generations they had followed the new places from North Carolina to the Mid West to Texas and finally to California.

After Mrs. Coffman's second marriage she and the children were alone, because her husband was in medical school in Philadelphia. Unfortunately the commodity known as money was something they hadn't much of.

Then suddenly ill health came to plague her. That was in the days when doctors treated incipient tuberculosis with altitude, and lots of it. They told her to get above 5000 feet, and stay there.

So she took her little money and her two boys and went up on old Mt. San Jacinto, where she got cheap accommodations in a private home.

She stayed up there four months, and her tuberculosis was cured forever. Also up there her entire career was mapped, altho she didn't know it at the time. The family cook did it.

This cook kept talking about a village down on the desert called Palm Springs where she went every winter when it got too cold on the mountain.

The cook was an uneducated woman, but her powers of description were so vivid and her enthusiasm was so catching that Mrs. Coffman took a vow that some day she would see this fabulous little village. The year was 1898. She didn't see Palm Springs until 10 years later.

She came down off the mountain a well woman. Her husand finished medical school and set up practice in Santa Monica. For a decade Mrs. Coffman was a mother and housewife.

But gradually the dampness and "gray days" of the coastline began to get on her nerves. It finally became an obsession with her, and once more she had to get away to preserve herself.

Finally she made her long- delayed trip to Palm Springs. As soon as she saw this desert, she knew she was here forever. Here the sun shone, both out out the sky and within herself.

She made a plan. She would start an inn or boarding house for people on holiday from Los Angeles. She went back and laid the plan before her father, who had moved to Los Angeles in the '80s.

And so in the fall of 1909 Mrs. Coffman and her husband and her two boys came to Palm Springs. The village consisted of 13 houses, 11 white people and 56 Indians.

It would be two years before the first auto arrived. It was six miles to the railroad, and they made the trip to the depot for supplies in a spring wagon.

There was no water pressure in the town, no electricity, no gas, no phone. Everybody had his own cow, including the Coffmans. People did their own washing.

"You could have bought 10 square miles, including the town, for $50,000," Mrs. Coffman told me. Today there are single lots you couldn't buy for that.

Mrs. Coffman opened her establishment for guests on Oct. 16, 1909. She had seven rooms. Three were in a frame house; four were in a converted barn. They weren't much, but they were clean. She waited a whole month before her first guest came.

She charged him $5 a day for room and board, and she did most of the work herself. Today a single guest pays from $12 to $30 a day, and, Mrs. Coffman hires 200 people to see that he is properly pampered.

– March 26, 1942

SILENT SAND DUNE SERMONS

PALM SPRINGS, Calif.—For eight years Mrs. Nellie Coffman hung onto Palm Springs like a stubborn dog clinging to a stick. If she hadn't done so, you never would have heard of the place.

From 1909 to 1917 her effort to run a resort hotel way out here on the desert was a touch-and-go affair. A few people came, but most people didn't.

Mrs. Coffman worked day and night. She kept books just like a farmer—she had two spikes, one for paid bills, the other for unpaid. At the end of each winter season, the unpaid stack was always the higher.

The Coffmans had some real estate in Santa Monica. Piece by piece this was sold to meet the bills at the end of each unsuccessful season on the desert.

Nobody had any faith in the thing but Mrs. Coffman. Today she gives the bulk of the credit to the two boys. But they themselves admit they couldn't see it, and anyhow they were away most of those tough early years, in school and then thru the first war.

Dr. Coffman, who was running the sanitarium end of the thing in a tent colony, also could not vision the day when people would flock to the desert. He held on a few years, and then went back to the coast. Mrs. Coffman was on her own.

Thru all those years she wouldn't give up. Her son Earl says of her today, "I don't know whether it was Mother's ability to see ahead, or just her plain stubbornness, that made her hang on. Probably a little of both."

But hang on she did, and in 1917 things began to break her way. The virtues of Palm Springs had begun to get about the country by word of mouth. People began to hear of the quiet and restfulness of the desert, of the winter sunshine, of Mrs. Coffman's little Desert Inn.

In 1917 the new crop of war millionaires looked afield for vacation places, and came to Palm Springs. And eastern families of old riches, cut off from Europe for the first time, also came. But most of all, the flu epidemic filled the place up.

Palm Springs kept itself without a flu death in the World War. Those that did get flu were immediately isolated. Los Angeles physicians sent their families to Palm Springs for safety. Everything was crowded. Everybody worked himself to death. In those days Mrs. Coffman worked until she felt she couldn't keep going. She was all alone now, too.

That was the toughest time, the crisis. And it was then that her beloved desert sustained her.

Mrs. Coffman is not a dreamy woman, or one given to fancy flights of soul-soaring, but she is a person of fine sensitivities—the kind who can draw courage from a flower or a thunderstorm. And her greatest strength and solace came from her love of the desert.

"In those terrible days in 1918," she says, "almost every evening just before sunset I'd go to a big sand mound south of town, and just sit there alone for about three-quarters of an hour, feeling the desert. Of course, I didn't go every day, you know, but every time I could, I went. And I think that's what pulled me thru."

To see her now—always cheerful, always friendly—you'd never guess she was once a melancholy and depressed kind of person. She was before she came to the desert. Even now, when she goes to the coast on trips, the corners of her mouth go down and she's a changed person. She is happy only in the desert.

The first auto came to Palm Springs two years after Mrs. Coffman arrived. She says the unreliability of autos was all that kept her going for years.

"Seems like they were always getting out of whack," she says. (She'd almost have to come from Indiana to use that expression "out of whack.")

"They'd get this far and then they'd get out of whack. It would take three weeks to get parts out from Los Angeles. The people would stay a few days, then take the train to the city, then in a couple of weeks come back for the machine. That way we got two cracks at them."

Things started going more rapidly after 1918. The two boys came home from that war, took a look, and saw what was about to happen. They went into business with their mother, and the three of them within the next decade built the tremendous Desert Inn as it is today—an investment of a million and a half.

In the afternoons you'll find her around the lobby or the grounds most of the time. She loves to talk with the guests. "I'll talk to anybody who'll listen to me," she says.

– March 27, 1942

LESSONS FROM NELLIE COFFMAN

PALM SPRINGS, Calif.—Mrs. Nellie Coffman's success in life—as the woman who started the era of desert resorts and has kept on top of the heap—is a marvelous example of two things:

1. That you don't have to follow your original ambition to be successful; that you can fit yourself to circumstances and still lead a wonderful life.

2. That it's never too late to start. For, as I've said, Mrs. Coffman was 42 when she began her second life (and on "half a shoestring," as she says), and she was past 50 before any real accomplishment came to her.

When she was young Nellie Coffman's one goal was music. She thought she had a fine voice, and maybe she did. Even during her first marriage she taught music. But finally she had to give her music up, and it didn't kill her.

In those "music" days, she often said to herself that, if she were ever thrown out on her own and had to make her own living, she was positive of one thing—she'd never do it by running a boarding-house.

"How the Lord must have sat back and laughed when He heard that remark," she says. For that's just what she's been going for 33 years. But now, if she had her entire life to live over, she'd have it exactly as it was.

Once into it, Mrs. Coffman found "running a boarding-house" a very engaging way to make a living. For she loves people and she always liked to keep house. "I love to scrub a floor," she says. Altho she has 200 employes, she still does most of the work in her own cottage on the grounds of the Desert Inn.

She is deeply interested in her employes; in fact, sort of mothers them. It is illustrated in the stories of her Filipino boys who have gone to war. Already 11 have enlisted, and when the Inn closes in May for the summer there will be around 30.

Mrs. Coffman is so proud of her boy Segundo Rigonan she could bust. He worked at the Inn for 12 years, and for the last three had no special duties at all. He drove Mrs. Coffman's car and spent the rest of the time as a "free agent," keeping an eye on things.

Segundo was the first to enlist. He was all hot for getting at the Japs. He wanted to kill a few personally. Several of the other boys followed him. Mrs. Coffman didn't try to dissuade them. In fact it made her prouder of them.

Segundo is already a sergeant, and when he gets leave he comes "home" to the Inn. One of the others boys was "home" during my visit. They go right to Mrs. Coffman's door the first thing.

Each week Mrs. Coffman sends them a box of stuff. Once she sent Segundo a box of dates. He wrote back that he was quartered with a bunch of Texans, and that they sure did like those dates.

So Mrs. Coffman, who is still fond of Texas, sent another box of 15 pounds, with a note to Segundo saying, "Get those longhorns' stomachs filled up."

Another of her Filipino boys is at Ft. Sill, Okla. The other day he wrote and said he'd sure like some of those cookies they used to serve at the Inn called "macaroons." So Mrs. Coffman had 600 macaroons baked and shipped them off to Ft. Sill.

Unlike most people, Mrs. Coffman doesn't think the war is going to bring the world to an end, altho she does think we'd better start changing our way of life pretty fast if we're going to win. She believes the hardships will strengthen our fiber, harden us up, force us to have more initiative. She, herself, wouldn't be afraid to start from scratch again at 75.

And war restrictions aren't bothering her, either. Like me, she believes in a philosophy of not laying away a lot of stuff (altho she did confess to buying a dollar's worth of hairpins) . But when everybody else was buying silk stockings, she didn't.

"I'll wear cotton stockings or go bare-legged," she says. "You know, the college girls think they started the fad of going bare-legged, but they didn't. I started it myself, 30 years ago, because I couldn't affords stockings at all, and because it was too hot out here in the summer to wear them anyhow."

The other day Mrs. Coffman was walking thru the grounds, and one of her workmen stopped her. He was a carpenter who had been here many years. He was gravely worried about what would happen to the resort business next year, and of course about his own job.

"Mrs. Coffman," he said, "you can see ahead about these things. What you think we'll be doing this time next year?"

Mrs. Coffman pretends to be no seer. But she doesn't worry too much, either. She figures that if everything comes to the worst she'll have a hell of a lot of company. So she said:

"John, I have no idea what we'll be doing. Maybe I'll be running a hash-house, for all I know. But, if I am, I bet I'll be cooking the best hash in town."

And she wasn't just talking thru her hat, either.

— March 28, 1942

COL. PYLE SALUTES

PALM SPRINGS, Calif.—This is the last of my pieces on Mrs. Nellie Coffman, the woman who mothered the bare deserts of the Southwest into a national haven for the tired and the vacation-hungry, who made it pay handsomely.

This is probably the most that has ever been written about her. For despite her friendly nature, Mother Coffman is very shy of publicity. (Of course, when I started working my cobra-like charms on her, she was helpless.) She has good reason to be shy. For, some years ago, a national magazine wrote her up and pictured her as a sort of Klondike Annie, with a muleskinner's tongue and knots on her fists.

Such a picture is very far from the truth. She could much more aptly be compared with my own mother. She has had a hard life, but there is nothing hard about her personality. As her son Earl says, "There has never been anything undignified about my mother."

Mother Coffman is a medium heavy woman, wears a net over her hair, still has her own teeth, and wears gold-rimmed spectacles. She does not look like a city woman when she's dressed up, nor does she look like a desert-rat, either. She looks like a midwestern grandmother.

She has never gone in for the baubles that many well-to-do people amuse themselves with. Her work has been her amusement. She is no slave to her work, but her facile mind, always thinking up something new to accomplish, has kept her young.

She does indulge herself by having breakfast in bed, but she has it at the atrocious hour of 6:30 a.m. In fact she has the bad habit of waking at 4 o'clock, and between then and breakfast time lying there and mulling over her business. There is an unwritten rule at the Desert Inn that any employe may come right into her room any time after 7 to discuss things with her.

Despite the vast grassy haven inside the grounds of the Inn, the Coffmans are still close to their greatest love—the desert. Walk a few blocks and you're out on the sand, away from everything.

Mrs. Coffman used to walk 20 miles a day, just because she loved to walk, but she goes mostly by car now. She says she'll be glad when her tires run out so she'll have to walk again. She feels better when she walks.

Because of the terrific heat (sometimes up to 120°) Palm Springs becomes practically a ghost town in summertime, with everybody gone and stores and houses boarded up.

But for the first 16 years Mrs. Coffman stayed right here thru the summer, because she was too poor to get out. Now she has a place up in the hills above Banning—not so very far away—where she goes for the summer. She calls the place "Lazy Acres."

Mrs. Coffman's devotion to the desert has been transmitted to her sons. Earl was telling me the other day about something that happened to him. Shortly after he was out of school he went to New York and got a job on Wall Street. The last war ended that, and he never went back.

But last summer he took an auto trip across the continent, and looked up his old Wall Street friends. He found many of them pretty threadbare, but some had gone on up to riches and the permanent life of high finance.

"But Good Lord, their outlook on life!" says Earl. "Worried and cynical and harassed. I never saw such gloom. You'd think nothing existed west of the Hudson. I had to drive clear to Tennessee before I could get it out of my system."

As I said before, Mrs. Coffman loves to gab with the guests. Yet, oddly enough for one in her business, she can't remember names. She has actually taken memory courses, and concentrated on the old connect-it-with-something-else system. But it was no go. She can't remember anybody's name until he has been her guest several weeks.

Before I arrived, some mail had come for me facetiously addressed to "Col. Pyle." Apparently the clerks tipped her off, for Mrs. Coffman greeted me as "Col. Pyle," and kept calling me that (she forgot my name later however.)

So, after a while I began to get self-conscious about the colonel business, and told her not to be too grave about it, me just being an honorary New Mexico colonel. Whereupon she laughed and said, "Why I'm a New Mexico colonel, too!" So we saluted, and now I call her "Col. Coffman."

She was, in addition, a Virginia colonel for a few months, until they sent her a bill for $25. So she "resigned" and sent her commission back.

Mrs. Coffman has not traveled a great deal, altho she did take a trip to the Orient seven years ago. She was enchanted by Japan, and can't quite conceive how such seemingly nice people could turn out to be such bad people.

— March 30, 1942

ERNIE IS A FRIEND OF A QUEEN

PALM SPRINGS, Calif.—It happens that, in addition to the many signal honors that have come to me—such as being frequently mistaken for a poet—I am also blessed with being a personal friend of the most popular girl in this popular desert resort.

She is the queen of this year's annual desert circus. She is referred to in the newspapers as "the tops in local royalty." Everybody is nuts about her. But having known her and her whole family for some years, I just treat her like dirt, which gives me a terrific sense of superiority over the rest of the population.

This girl's name is Edie Bush. She is 21 years old (and purty, too). Despite my superior airs toward her, I make it a point in a sort of underhand way to court her good-will, because by the time she's 40 she's going to own this whole damn place, and 20 years from now I may be needing a nickel for a cup of coffee.

Edie is hostess at the Deep Well Ranch where I've been staying (in fact, that's why I've been staying there). If it would interest you, I'll tell you how such things as this come about. If I had time I'd make a novel out of it.

Well, some five years ago I was going down the Yukon River on a paddle-wheel steamboat. That sounds pretty romantic, but it was cold and the mosquitoes were terrible, and anyhow Edie wasn't on the boat, so don't get ahead of your story.

But on this boat I met a couple from San Francisco—Duane and Sevigne Bush—and we became good friends. I stayed with them at their gold camp in Alaska and visited their home on our return to the States.

The following winter there came to this couple a beautiful baby daughter named Vondre, a remarkable child, and for some mysterious reason I was appointed godfather to same.

In the ensuing years I have cultivated this child with perfumes, candy, gardenias, love letters, old lace and an occasional pinch, and have finally made such an impression upon her that now, at the age of 4, she actually remembers my name.

In the course of this courtship of my god-daughter, I naturally met the rest of her family including my god-daughter's elder sister, Edie (now 21 and putry—or am I getting old and repetitious?) But anyhow, I met her, and then she went off to Oregon to college.

After three years of higher learning she decided her time had come, so she turned her back upon the classroom and looked about for something to conquer. And since her Cousin Melba rather runs the Deep Well Guest Ranch, she chose that as her first conquest.

She didn't choose wrong. In one season she has captured the whole place. Everybody in town knows her, from Mother Coffman down to the lowliest cowboy. She walks gaily into the snooty Racquet Club in her overalls as if she owned the place, and they hold out their arms.

She hasn't been out of overalls since last October, and dreads the near day when she will have to return to San Francisco and put on a dress. She wears her hair in pigtails, and guests can't believe she is more than 15. That saves her a lot of trouble, too.

She plays miserable paddle-tennis (I beat her, 6-2, and me with athlete's foot) and she's lousy at dominos, but she's got what it takes to make the guests happy. She has a crush on the word "wonderful." If a disgruntled guest were to come up foaming and yell, "This place stinks!" I'm sure Edie would say, "Wonderful, Mr. Nibbs," and he would be whipped.

Edie smokes cigarets, used to take a cocktail but doesn't any more, and keeps her overall pockets full of string and nails and things like a little boy. She knows her way about the world, and yet there are a lot of bad things she hasn't learned yet.

For instance, one day coming from town in the station wagon, one of the ranch's women guests got mad at something and told Edie and the other girl hostess off in a manner considerably unbecoming to a lady. The girls arrived at the ranch practically in tears.

So Frank Bennett tried to get out of them what had happened and just what the woman had called them, and finally they told him, but neither of them knew what the words meant. And Frank said to them, "It's a hell of a lot of good three years of college did you girls. You don't even know all the words." (The vulgar guest left next morning, by request.)

In the big Palm Springs annual circus, Edie will ride (or has ridden by the time this appears) on the leading float surrounded by her "court" of five girls. I wish I could have been there, to swell with pride. But a man can't have everything, and I've already had my inning—walking nonchalantly down the main street of Palm Springs with overalled Miss Bush on my arm, the cynosure of all eyes, as they say. It was "wonderful."

– April 3, 1942

PALM SPRINGS REPORT

PALM SPRINGS, Calif.—Most of my time in Palm Springs has been taken up with work, but I did have one afternoon off to look around a little.

And I was amazed at the number of very lovely places to stay. There are scores of places that make your mouth water. I'd like to stay a year and try them all.

They're all built on the same plan—very low and spread out, so the sun can get in. Actually, they're like tourist courts, except they're super-modern and set amidst beautiful lawns dotted with bright-colored umbrellas and low chairs, and nearly all have their private swimming pools.

Altho my purpose in coming here was to write about Mother Coffman and the Desert Inn, there is one other place that runs neck and neck. That is the Hotel El Mirador.

It is built on the same plan as the Inn—vastly spread out. It was built in 1928, and launched with a gigantic wave of movie-star publicity.

The Mirador and Desert Inn are the same size, and their rates are the same. The Mirador is flashier, but they cater to the same class of solid wealth.

Altho most visitors to Palm Springs actually come only to rest and get a good shot of sunshine, it was the idea of Hollywood pulchritude out here that finally made Palm Springs known to every cow-puncher and telephone girl in America.

It's funny how people go silly over publicized beauty. Visitors stare their eyes out looking for Dorothy Lamour or Marlene Dietrich. But, if the guests at the Mirador, for instance, would just look around a bit, they'd find a very satisfactory substitute.

I mean Miss Janette Grant, the Mirador's publicity director. Her main interest in life is journalism. But I've taken an option on her anyhow, just in case Hollywood starts nosing around.

One afternoon I went with friends to the Racquet Club. This is a very flossy place, open only to members and their guests. They have room for only 12 people to stay there, but scores come in the afternoon to play tennis or swim, or sit and drink .

The club is run by Charles Farrell, the former movie actor who used to always play opposite Janet Gaynor. It is a favorite hangout for the movie people.

The afternoon I was there I learned that the lady in white shorts and lots of lipstick at the next table was none other than Miss Rita Hayworth. I didn't take a pulse count on her, but she did appear thrilled to be sitting so close to me.

Palm Springs is considered sort of a haven from Jap bombers, because it's back behind the treacherous mountains, and there's nothing remotely resembling a military objective here. If the Japs bombed Palm Springs it would be just pure orneriness.

Consequently, people have started sending Mother Coffman their treasured possessions for her to store until after the war. One woman has sent her three boxes of fine china. And Mrs. Coffman's sister, in Santa Monica, has sent all her treasured Indian baskets.

"Why that's silly," Mrs. Coffman told her, "to send the baskets and not come yourself. Nobody but you cares anything about those old baskets, so why save them if you get killed?"

And her sister replied, "Well, I just love them so much I can't bear to think of them falling into Japanese hands after I'm gone."

Mother Coffman, in addition to everything else, is a poet—or a rhymester, as she says.

The Inn is given to leaving little printed jingles around the rooms, all decorated up with red sketches, to explain things to the guests. And I learned to my astonishment that Mother Coffman writes them herself—thinks them up at night when she can't sleep.

The latest one is entitled "Sherman was right. War IS hell." And the poem says:

> "Please don't scold the maid, she's not to blame—
> You're short on towels, and that's a shame
> But Uncle Sammy, brave and wise,
> Has asked us to economize.
> If this restriction leaves you numb,
> Wait'll we tackle sugar, chum!"

So, because of this restriction, I've had to try keeping clean with only five hand towels, three bath towels, two wash rags and a bath mat each day. A man just can't do it, that's all. So I'm leaving, before the garbage man starts chasing me.

— April 4, 1942

ERNIE'S LONG JUMP

PHOENIX, Ariz.—It's a long jump from Palm Springs to Phoenix, but when I jump, I jump big.

Breaking away from California is sort of like pulling your boot out of the mud. You can't do it gradually. You have to heave.

It was hard for me to leave California, for I have developed a very great affection for the place. I suppose it's the farmer in me, but I've long passed the day when I can sneer sophisticatedly either at Hollywood or the climate. I like them both.

Now I'm headed east.

Business is certainly good this year in the desert. I had intended stopping over a few days at Yuma, but couldn't even get a place to lay my head.

It was the same story in Phoenix. We got in after dark and couldn't get a hotel room even tho I had phoned ahead. Finally I just sat down in the lobby of the Hotel Westward Ho and started to cry. So they took pity and dug me up a room in a private club.

In Phoenix and Tucson, the tourist season has been as good as ever—maybe a little better. Many people have come to the desert who otherwise would have gone to California on their vacations. And, too, lots of Californians have come inland—just in case. They say that two-thirds of the traffic these days is eastbound.

Coming across, I picked up a soldier, and asked him how far he was going. "Just as far as you are," he said.

"I'm going to New York," I said, "but it'll take me about two months to get there."

"Well, I'll get off at Dallas," the soldier said.

He was on six-day leave, hitch-hiking clear from the Coast to Dallas to get married. He figured he could make it in 48 hours each way, which would give him two days at home.

He had been in the Army six months and liked it all right. He was a bank teller before he joined up—so the Army made a pill-roller out of him, a medical attendant.

When we crossed the Colorado River at Yuma, Army entries stopped us. They only stop cars in which service men are riding. They wanted to check my soldier's furlough papers.

They were o.k., so the guard said, "All right, roll up your windows and cross the bridge."

When we got on the Arizona side and stopped at the Arigicultural Inspection Station, I asked the inspector why we had been told to roll up our windows.

"Oh, it's the Army," the inspector said. "I've never been able to find out the reason."

I asked several people, and nobody knew why. Maybe I'm just too dumb to be roaming loose like this, but I can't make any sense out of such an order. If anybody knows, I wish he'd write and tell me.

In Phoenix there is a little restaurant, only about twice the size of your living room, where you can get a good meal for 40 cents or so. The place never closes.

On the window they have a sign saying: "A free meal to any person finding this cafe without a customer day or night."

I asked the cashier how often they had to give away a free meal.

"Well, when I worked here three years ago," she said, "we'd give away about two a year."

"But how about now?" I asked. "Surely between 2 and 5 in the morning there must be times when nobody's here."

"Oh, it's busier than ever then," she said. "We haven't had to give a free meal in ages. Why, between 2 and 5 in the morning it's so packed we can't even scrub the floor.'"

There's one Hollywood item still left in my system, before we get too far away.

A friend of mine out there recently saw Gene Autry, the Western star, and found out that Gene is due to be drafted in the early summer. And this friend spoke as follows:

"Gene's ready to go, but I think it's foolish for the Army to take a man like that. Here he is paying the Government a quarter of a million a year in taxes. When he goes in the Army that revenue will stop. Don't you think that's penny wise and pound foolish?"

The question stopped me. I'd never even thought of anything like that before. Is that a sound theory or not? It does seem sensible at first, but there must be a flaw in it somewhere.

– April 6, 1942

ERNEST TAYLOR PYLE

Ernest Taylor (Ernie) Pyle was born in the little farming community of Dana, Indiana, August 3, 1900. He grew up in this environment, and later attended the University of Indiana. Then he became a cub reporter on the La Porte (Indiana) Herald, and went on from there to work on newspapers in Washington, D.C.

When World War II began he was a recognized national columnist for the Scripps-Howard newspaper chain, and his material appeared in more than 200 publications. He became a war correspondent, and won immediate added laurels for the insight and warmth of his stories about the American fighting man. He won the Pulitzer Prize for his dispatches in 1944.

He was killed by a Japanese bullet April 18, 1945, on the tiny South Pacific island of Ie Shima. He is buried in Punchbowl Memorial Cemetery in Hawaii.

Lt. General Omar Bradley, (left), General Dwight Eisenhower, and Ernie Pyle in his war correspondent's uniform, in France.